it Seems to Me

ELEANOR ROOSEVELT

W · W · NORTON & COMPANY · INC · New York

Contents

Preface

This collection of questions and answers has been taken from the monthly pages which I have done over a long period of years, first for Ladies' Home Journal and now for McCall's magazine. The questions are chosen by the magazine from letters that come to me through their office. Sometimes if there is a particular interest in one subject, they will take the substance of a good many letters and make it into one question but all the questions are taken from letters addressed to me by individuals, in care of the magazine. I have never made the choice among the questions that should be answered. That has always been done by the magazine. Sometimes when they feel a question is not suitable for answer in the magazine, they will forward it to me. Every two weeks, therefore, I get a large envelope filled with letters and I answer them separately, so I not only have contact with people through the pages of the magazine but I frequently have contact with people where their individual letters seem possible to answer.

The material in this book has been classed under twenty-four different headings and an effort has been made to cover a great variety of the questions which have been sent in to me. It has always interested me to find what a vast coverage of human interest one can get by simply trying to answer the questions sent in for a feature of this kind. This is not a book that anyone will want to read straight through because there is no narrative but many people may find it interesting to read pieces of it now and then.

I have often been surprised by the number of letters which would come to me in regard to certain answers I had given. Sometimes people disagree and most of us find that those who disagree are more prone to write than those who agree but when I gave my definition of a mature person recently it brought me a great many letters saying that this particular answer was very helpful and that the writers constantly kept it before them. This was both a surprise and a pleasure.

I imagine it is easier for people to ask questions of someone who seems so remote that they will probably never see them, than it might be to ask questions of one's next door neighbor. That, I think, is what makes many of the questions deal with subjects that are of personal but also universal interest.

I love people and I love the contacts that these pages have brought me, remote contacts to be sure but still rather intimate ones. They are an enrichment of one's knowledge of human nature and the study of human beings is, I think, the most fascinating study in the world.

I hope this book may prove of interest to others and may be helpful in the same way that I hope my pages in McCall's magazine may continue to be both helpful and enjoyable to the many readers who occasionally write me that it is the first page they turn to when their magazine arrives.

Eleanor Roosevelt

it Seems to Me {

1. on Growing Up

I am eleven and a half and like to listen to mystery stories on the radio. My mother and father object because they are too exciting and limit me to one a day. I would like your opinion, please.

> I think your mother and father are very wise. What do you really get out of mystery stories? They give you a certain amount of excitement, but they do not give you anything that you want to keep in your mind.

I am thirteen years of age and in junior high school. I like very much to go out and have fun with the girls, but my mother taught me it was wrong to yell on the street and call attention to myself and flirt and whistle at boys I don't know. The only girls my age that I would care to run around with do these things. How could I still be friends with them and go places with them and yet not be the fun killer?

> I happen to have been brought up in an era which

thought that whistling and flirting with boys on the street was not done. I am afraid, therefore that, like your mother, I would feel a little bit uncomfortable in doing it. If you like the girls and still find pleasure in their company, even though you cannot do the kind of things they do, I suppose it will not bother them very much whether you act as they do or not. I rather think, however, that you will soon find that you are bored with both the girls and the kind of boys they are "picking up." You may find other friends who are more congenial and who meet their friends in other ways.

I am a girl of 13 of the Jewish faith. My mother and I have been discussing the problem of eventual dates with boys. My mother says I should confine my dates to Jewish boys. I say it does not matter with whom I go out, Jewish boys or boys of other religions. What should I do?

I do not like to answer questions on subjects which really have to be decided within a family. Racial and religious questions fall into that category, but I would point out to your mother that we have to live in a world in which all races and religions have to learn somehow to live together.

I am a girl of 13½. An only child, I get lonely. I want a dog. My mother won't give her consent. She doesn't like dogs. Can you tell me what to do?

I am afraid I cannot give you a formula for persuasion. Judging from my own experience as a mother, however, I am sure that if you try to please your mother in every way and prove to her that you are reliable and responsible, your mother will someday feel that she can trust

you to look after a dog and not to allow it to become a
burden on her.

*I am a girl, fifteen years of age, and in my sophomore
year in high school. I'm invited to go to the movies and
parties with boys who drive their own cars. My mother
does not approve and I, having read your column, suggested writing to you. She agreed and we both will abide
by your decisions.*

     I am rather an old lady to advise on this question, but I
think my daughter felt the way your mother does, and I
do not think she allowed her daughter, when she was
fifteen, to go to movies and parties where boys who were
not much older did the driving of the car. I think she
felt that a little later on there would be more judgment
which could not be expected at your age. In some states,
boys are not allowed to drive until they reach eighteen,
and then they cannot have a full license, except under
certain conditions. That is because, in the nature of
things, young people have less experience and less judgment. Put that down as one of the advantages that come
with age!

*I am a little over sixteen and am a high-school junior. I
like to dance, but am not allowed to go to any dances except school dances, two or three times a year. Also, my
mother dislikes me to go bowling. Do you think it is
wrong for high-school girls to go to bowling alleys?*

     I think your mother is a very wise woman. Sixteen is
very young. You do not realize it now, but you have
plenty of time ahead of you to go bowling and dancing.
Your health is important today, and if you do not have

all the experiences and all the pleasures at the age of six-teen which you desire, you will enjoy them much more when you are a couple of years older. What is more, the young men will find you more interesting because they will not have had a chance to get tired of you.

I will soon be seventeen years old and my parents won't let me have dates. They always want me to go along with them. It seems as if they don't trust their own child. When I go without them, they want me to take my kid sister along. How can I get them to understand it is my life, and I want to have some fun?

Your parents probably enjoy your company and want you with them and do not realize that you have reached an age where you want a life of your own to some extent. I doubt very much that they do not trust you. They are trying to safeguard you from being talked about unkindly and they know that if they are with you, or if your younger sister is on hand, no one can say that you did something which you did not do.

At seventeen, however, it is understandable that you should want to have your own dates, and I think proba-bly the best thing is for you to have a talk with your parents, explain the situation to them and learn from them what are the rules they want you to observe and then go ahead and have fun.

I am seventeen, a senior in high school, and have spent every one of my teen-age years in misery because of self-consciousness. I cannot look a person in the eye even to say "Hello" without getting a funny expression on my

face, and to give an oral report in school is almost torture.
Whenever anyone as much as glances at me, I feel as
though he is criticizing me. This bashfulness not only
causes me great unhappiness, but affects my marks. The
one and only thing I am looking forward to in life is mar-
rying and having a large family. I really love kids more
than any other thing in this world. And I realize my
dream will remain a dream if I do not snap out of this
present condition. Please, Mrs. Roosevelt, is there any
way I can do this?

> Surely. If you will just stop thinking about yourself and
> begin to think about other people, you can make them
> and yourself happier. You can help them if you can find
> something to do for them. If you like children, get some
> fun out of being with them and do not think about
> whether people are watching you or not. Believe me,
> when you think people are criticizing you, they proba-
> bly haven't even given you a thought. It is remarkable
> how unconscious most people are about other people.
> If you can just remember that, in starting out to do the
> kind things that any human being does who lets him-
> self be natural, you will soon make friends.

I am a senior in high school. What general advice would
you give a boy 17 about life?

> I am sure that all one can say has been said so many
> times to a boy of seventeen by his teachers, his parents
> and his pastor. I will not tell you the obvious things—
> that it is better to be honest and kind than to be dis-
> honest and selfish—but I will tell you that if you face
> life with a spirit of adventure and with courage you will

get more out of it than if you are timid and unimaginative.

One of my girl friends wanted to meet the boy I go with, or did go with, and so I got her a date with a friend of his. Now she is going with my boy friend and I am left holding the bag. How can I win him back?

> If I were you I would not try to win him back. If he can be taken away so easily, I do not think his affection is very deep. I would be inclined to find someone else whom I liked. Perhaps you will find that a new boy is really more attractive than the old one, and I should hope he might have a stronger character.

I guess you'll be rather surprised to hear from a boy, but I've got a problem. I am nineteen years old. My mother considers me a child and my father thinks I am as much of a man as he is. Isn't that a mess? I look at it this way. The Army thought I was old enough to go to war. Why am I a child at home? I went with a girl before I went overseas, and now I am starting out in a new and good job. I love her very much, and we would like to get married in a few months, but it would cause a complete eruption in my home. All I need is some way to make mother see the light and understand what I want to do.

> Nineteen is rather young to get married, though I realize that having been in the war and overseas, you are probably mature for your years. That may not, however, be the case with the girl, and possibly your mother is not so much disturbed because she thinks you are a child, as because she feels that both of you, in the course of the next few years or so, may change, as so often happens,

and then you might find you had made a mistake and were not as compatible as one should be in a life partnership. I think you have every right to demand that you be treated as a man at home, and be given freedom in every possible way; but if your mother asks you to wait a year, even though you are both anxious to get married and you have a good job, remember there are many years ahead of you. A man who marries, at twenty-one, a girl who is perhaps a year or two younger than himself still has a long period to enjoy the happiness which he has waited for. Of course I do not know what the special circumstances may be, and I am only giving you advice in a very general way, because in almost every case there are special reasons which might well change the point of view which a stranger like myself holds.

I would like to know your views on necking, petting, and so on, for teen-agers—or anyone, for that matter. Also late hours and good-night kisses. There have been many opinions expressed on this subject, but they all seem to beat around the bush so you don't know any more than when they started.

You must remember that I am sixty-nine years old and therefore "necking" and "petting" have very little charm for me! That holds good for good-night kisses! Seriously, however, I think a girl is wise if she does not make herself cheap. I know that it is ordinarily said that unless a girl allows a young man to kiss her or lets herself be handled with familiarity, dates are apt to be few and far between. I have always doubted that, because I have always thought a really nice young man would understand quite well that until a girl was really attracted to him, she did not care to be mauled, and that she could be just as good fun and just as informal and friendly without the type of demonstration which sometimes leads one into more than one had counted on.

I think, also, you have to remember that someday you are going to meet someone you care for a great deal, and then you may be sorry that you have given other people so much of what you would like to have kept for a really great love.

Would you mind giving me your definition of a mature person?

A mature person is one who does not think only in absolutes, who is able to be objective even when deeply stirred emotionally, who has learned that there is both good and bad in all people and in all things, and who walks humbly and deals charitably with the circumstances of life, knowing that in this world no one is all-knowing and therefore all of us need both love and charity.

2. on Getting Along with People

I have found that there are difficulties when one tries to follow the splendid advice of Polonius: "This above all, to thine own self be true." Do you believe that, for a young wife and mother who wants to live at peace with her neighbors and community, it is sometimes wisest to avoid voicing a belief which, though she may feel strongly about it, would differ so from what is "accepted" locally that it would cause comment or worse? I refer to such things as race prejudice and topics involving basic ideas on labor and capital. Often I've been part of a group when these topics came up and, though I knew the futility of trying to change others' views, couldn't help speaking my own, leading me only into the feeling of being looked down on or set apart. For one who wants to live a quiet home life, do you think that the hypocrisy involved in keeping quiet is justified?

It seems to me that it is not hypocrisy to keep quiet

unless you are asked a direct question. If you are asked a direct question, then I think it is better as briefly as possible to state your own point of view, doing it in as conciliatory a way as possible. If you live in a neighborhood where the ideas of your neighbors differ radically from your own, it is probably better for you and your husband if you try not to force your ideas down others' throats. Live your life according to your own lights and they will come to know how you feel, and in the end they will respect you.

Immediately after graduation from college, I married and came to a strange town to live. Within a year our child was born. Now that the baby is a year old I find myself with some spare time occasionally. I have met some very nice people through our church, but am too shy to be a good mixer. Still, I would like to be a more active member of this community. I was educated to be a teacher and feel that I could and should contribute something to the welfare of those outside my own family circle. How does one get to be a member of clubs and organizations?

If I were you I would take an immediate interest in the parent-teachers association. Your child will be going to nursery school or kindergarten before long, and you might take an interest now in the school facilities in your community. I think you will find that that will lead to your joining other organizations. Perhaps in connection with your husband's business there are certain groups to which other women belong, which you could enjoy too.

Do you think a friend of several years' standing should
feel free to drop in unannounced and bring friends with
her whenever she feels like it?

I think it is the right of every individual to give his
friends whatever privileges he wishes them to have. One
creates the rules by which one lives with one's friends.
If you have a relationship in which a friend feels free
to drop in unannounced and bring friends, then I should
think it quite all right for a friend to do so. If, however,
you do not like it, that is something you should explain,
because such intimacy grows, and it grows by mutual
consent. If it is disagreeable to you it will eventually end
your friendship.

I have the great fortune of being able to go to California
for my vacation to some relatives of my mother. These
people are Catholic, and I am High Church of England.
I would hate to miss church when I am on my vacation.
Should I go to the Catholic church with them, and say
nothing? I have never visited relatives and don't want
to start a feud for nothing. I am twenty-three years old.

If your relatives live in a city, there is no reason why
you should not attend your own church which in this
country would be the Episcopal Church. If you will be
living in some area where churches are difficult to reach,
and the rest of the family drives to a Catholic church
and there is no way of your getting to your own church,
it is purely optional whether you wish to go with them
or not to go at all. No one will be offended if you say
you prefer to go to your own church. At twenty-three
you are a grown person and not a child.

What do you think are the three most important requisites for happiness?

A feeling that you have been honest with yourself and with those around you; a feeling that you have done the best you could both in your personal life and in your work; and the ability to love others.

Have you ever told a "white lie"? Do you think that white lies are ever justifiable?

If what you mean by a "white lie" is such pleasant things as one says casually in social relationships—for instance, saying to someone when you meet that it is a pleasure to see them, when you really have no idea whether it is going to be a pleasure or not, or telling people when you refuse an invitation that you are refusing because of a previous engagement when you are not willing to give the real reason—I certainly have told white lies and I do think they are justified.

I am twenty-two and an unusually shy person. I am attractive enough and have nice clothes and I definitely am not conceited, but I don't seem to have nearly as many friends as those who are less fortunate than I. Please advise.

I really cannot advise you except to say that if you would stop worrying about yourself and think about others, and give them a good time, you probably would find yourself gathering more friends around you, and before you knew it you would have as many friends as you wanted.

Please tell me where all the social clubs everyone speaks of are located. I am in my late 20's, dress well and am

*attractive, yet so lonely I don't think I can stand it much
longer. Any suggestions you can give me will be gratefully
received.*

I do not know that giving you the address of clubs about
town would do you any good, but if I were you I would
join the Y.W.C.A., where you would find yourself drawn
into groups of people your own age; or you could join
with some of the groups working in your church, which
would also put you in touch with social groups. I should
think if you are working anywhere you should make
friends among the people with whom you work and
create some social life for yourself in that way.

*My son and his wife are Republicans, but my daughter
recently married a man who favors the Democrats. No
matter how hard I try I can't keep the two couples from
getting into nasty political arguments. It ruins all their
visits with me. Tell me, please, how do you handle political differences in your family?*

I try to make them amusing. We have vast differences in
our family. All of them love to argue. They can argue
passionately about things they do not care about, and
anyone who did not know them would think they were
about to kill one another. But I find a little laughter and
teasing and, if necessary, arbitrarily changing the subject
make our family gatherings rather entertaining.

*Somewhere I read that you had a real inferiority complex
or something of the sort when you were a young girl, and
I would like to know how you overcame it.*

Yes, I had an inferiority complex, which lasted during
many years of my young married life and isn't completely

gone today. I suppose it was the force of circumstances that made me overcome it. There were certain things I had to do whether I liked doing them or not, and no matter how badly I did them I had to go through with them. More and more I have had to think about other people, and that always helps one to forget oneself.

If you had your choice, would you prefer being a hostess or a guest?

I am afraid I prefer being hostess. It is so much easier to have people visit you than to go to them. But that is selfish, I suppose—and it is also true that I have enjoyed being a guest a great many times.

3. on Love and Courtship

*Do you agree that a girl should hide her intellectual side
if she's going to be popular with boys?*

No. What is the use of being liked by people whom you
do not like? If you hide the things in which you are
really interested in order to please people of different
interests, you are not going to have friends with whom
you can be natural, and that seems to me a very foolish
way to live. I think, however, that if a girl boasts of her
knowledge everyone will laugh at her. Just be perfectly
natural and talk about the things that interest you with
people who have similar interests. Then you will have
friends that you will enjoy and who will enjoy you.

*Would you please tell me if you believe, as I do, in love
at first sight? Do you know of any actual cases?*

No, I do not know of any actual cases, and I do not
know whether I believe in love at first sight or not. I
have seen love develop very quickly between two people

and I have heard people say that they knew the minute they found themselves with the man or woman whom they later married, that there was immediately a great attraction, but I haven't the faintest idea if it was love at first sight or not.

Don't you think a girl can say "no" and turn away the attentions of a man? A girl I know stole a boy friend I was going steady with. She is telling everybody that she just couldn't help it. Don't you think she ought to have played fair and kept hands off? I know you can say "no" to a man, because I have, and he knew I meant it.

Yes, you can say "no" to a man and you can send him away; but, my dear child, remember that if you were "going steady" with a young man, and any girl could take him away, then his heart was not yours anyway. You could not have held him, and if this girl had not taken him, some other girl would. You are both better off to discover before marriage that on his part, at least, love was not lasting.

Please give me some advice in regard to necking. I will be twenty-five in two months, I am an only child, live with my parents, am considered nice-looking, and rather shy. I have been a stenographer for three years and I am a church member. I have only dated five boys several times and each date ended in a necking bout. Is necking something that everyone does and no one admits? Do girls who refuse to neck ever get married?

My dear young lady, I think you are not very grown up in spite of your twenty-five years. I would advise you to have a few more dates and perhaps you will find among your friends boys who do not insist on necking. Probably most girls today have had some necking experiences, but I do not think that really has anything to do with whether you get married or not.

My best friend, who is an attractive blonde, is losing all interest in life because of a certain fellow. It has been a year since they broke up. He doesn't seem to want to bother with her any more. How can I help her overcome her feeling for him, or advise her how to get him back again?

I think you had better be a little careful about interfering, even with your best friend. She would probably resent it, and in all probability time is what is needed to solve her problem.

My mother and I disagree sharply in our judgment of people. How important, under the circumstances, should it be to have my mother approve of the man I marry?

This is a very difficult question, as it involves the feeling that you have for your mother. If it is very close, and if you are devoted to her, I think you will find that you will be able to interpret the man you marry to her and change her point of view. It is always well to weigh the opinion of older people, because they have had more experience than you possibly can have. However, you are the one who is going to marry the man and live with him, and so ultimately it will have to be your decision. I would not hurry, however, and I would make every possible effort to bring about unity in the family, since the break between the home of the past and the one you hope to make is always a sad and upsetting experience.

Would you advise a girl to marry a man who has just returned from overseas as soon as possible, or should she wait five or six months until he is settled in civilian life?

That is a personal question which everyone, I think, has to decide for herself. If you marry a man who has just returned from overseas, you will know you are going to have not only the usual period of adjustment which comes in every marriage, but the added adjustment which every man must make on his return to civilian life. If a woman truly loves a man, however, and fully understands what she is doing, she may feel that they can work out their new life better together than apart, but that is something they have to decide and no one can decide it for them.

To some people, love is near-passion; to some, a quiet understanding; to others, a more complex concoction. Will you give me a definition with your own list of ingredients?

Love can have all the things you mention and a good many more. One could write books on the subject, but I think it is perhaps easier to read those already written. Certainly there is no lack of definitions far better than I could give. Why not start off with the Sonnets from the Portuguese, by Elizabeth Barrett Browning, and then go on through almost all the poets? You will find that from the earliest days down to the present, love has been an unending theme.

*I am a college girl and belong to a well-to-do family, but
I am extremely unattractive. I have never had suitors and
realize my chances are very slim. With this in view, what
attitude should I adopt toward life?*

> For heaven's sake, my dear child, do not make up your
> mind because you are in college and haven't had any
> suitors that you are unattractive. Looks alone do not
> make one attractive. I do not know you, so I do not
> know just how to answer your question, but remember
> that one can do a great deal to improve one's personal
> appearance. The most important thing is what comes
> from the inside out. If you cultivate your mind and your
> spirit, you can have charm, which is far more important
> than looks. You may not have suitors today, but do not
> try too hard to have them. If you become an interesting
> and charming person, that will appeal to people and
> draw them to you when you are out of college and have
> a chance to make your place in the world.

*I am in love with a man 15 years my senior. We agree
upon most things of importance and are very happy together. Yet he is skeptical about marriage because of the
many people who insist it won't work out. As far as I
am concerned age does not make any difference as long
as we love each other and hold the same interests. Do
you agree?*

> While I think such a difference in age may prove a
> hardship for a woman in her marriage at some point
> in later life, I think it does not create an insuperable
> barrier. I have known many happy marriages in which
> there was a great disparity in age. As long as the two
> people have similar interests I think there is a chance

of many years of happiness together. It is true that, later on, the woman may be left alone, or she may be in better health than her husband in the last years of his life, but a man of 60 is often quite as well and strong as a woman of 45, so I would not consider this difference in age a deciding factor.

4. on Marriage

I understand you once wrote down several rules for marital happiness. Will you tell me the chief ones please?

I cannot remember ever having indulged in this pastime, but if you heard that I did so perhaps I did. I must have been more rash than I am now, so I will not try to write down more than one or two suggestions, certainly not rules.

In all human relationships, and marriage is one of the most difficult, I think perhaps the important qualities for all individuals are unselfishness and flexibility. Tact can be a help also, and real love which occasionally carries you beyond interest in yourself is essential.

What do you think are the most difficult problems involved in marrying an only child?

The fact that as a rule an only child has been accustomed to being the center of the stage and may find it difficult to enter into a dual relationship where each partner is equal. Also the parents of an only child are apt to expect more consideration, since their whole interest has been centered in this child, and the adjustments to the new relationship are sometimes difficult.

My husband says he has a right to have an affair with another woman when he's overseas. When I ask him if I have the same kind of rights he says no, I'm the mother of children and have to be respectable. It's not that I want an affair with another man, but I don't think his attitude is right. Do you?

Of course what your husband is trying to guard against is the feeling of guilt which comes to any man who has been physically unfaithful to the woman whom he really loves and does not want to lose. The act of being physically unfaithful seems much less important to the average man, and he finds it hard to understand why the woman he loves looks upon it as all-important. Yet, as you prove by your question to him, if a woman tries to take the same point of view a husband is quite horrified and turns to the old code of respectability on the woman's part for the sake of the children. How about respectability on the man's part being of value to the children?

There is something more, however, that should be said on this whole question, since physical faithfulness is perhaps more difficult for men than for women. I imagine your husband, who apparently does love you, is trying to make sure that you will not turn away from him if anything of the kind should happen while he is overseas. You and he will have to decide what is the right attitude to take. Nobody else can decide it for you.

I married a widower. The first thing I saw when I entered my new home was the picture of his first wife prominently displayed on the mantelpiece. He still goes to the cemetery to mourn her, carrying flowers, especially on days meaningful to his first marriage. What is the sensible attitude for each of us to display?

When you married a widower you knew he had had a first wife. In all probability you hoped that he had loved his first wife, because the fact that he had been able to love her would make it probable that he would love you.

The fact that he is still loyal to her memory and still mourns her is something you should be happy about. If you had known her you probably would join with him in thinking of her. As long as you had not known her you cannot do that, but you can at least respect and admire him for his loyalty and realize that in a different way he will give you more just because of this loyalty.

No one loves two people in exactly the same way, but one may love two people equally and yet differently. And if you love one person very much you will love another person perhaps even more because you have learned how to love and what love can mean.

Be happy with your husband in the kind of love he gives you and be grateful for his loyalty to the past, because it augurs well for his loyalty to the present.

Do you think the number of children parents plan to have should be influenced by the family's income? After all, a man doesn't know how much he'll be making when his children reach college age, so how can he judge?

It probably isn't possible for a man to judge how much

he will be making when his children reach college age, but if he goes along and has children reasonably spaced, he is apt to have a fairly good idea of how he is getting on in the world.

I am a rather young housewife who for four years has been working to help my husband make a down payment on a little home. Do you think I could safely quit my job now and keep house as I have wanted to do all my life, or do you think that conditions in the future might be such that I'd better keep my job?

Not knowing you and your husband, it is a little difficult for me to decide just what conditions you mean. If you are talking about world conditions as a whole, I would tell you that nearly all people have to make such decisions as face you without too great a sense of security. Do you suppose our ancestors, when they decided to embark on the Mayflower, were sure what conditions they would meet in the future? It seems rather improbable.

If I were you, I would talk the situation over with your husband and decide what would give you the greatest sense of achievement and happiness. Then I would go ahead and do it and meet whatever comes in the future as best you can when it confronts you.

I was married three months ago, but up to this time I haven't made any new friends, because I'm just too shy. What can I do to stop feeling so uncomfortable with strangers?

Remember, first of all, that your husband fell in love with you and married you and that he is proud of you.

That should give you some assurance. Try to forget how you feel and think only of how your guests feel and your shyness will soon disappear.

Those who argue for "planned parenthood" point out that the size of the family should be limited for the sake of health and economics. Don't you think it is important, too, to limit the family so that there is enough of a mother's attention and affection to go around generously?

I do, but that is one of the things that intelligent advocates of planned parenthood have stressed, and it is part of all better health conditions, since many women have not the strength to give to the older children when they have too short periods of recuperation. This is not always true, however, since we have all known women who could have a child every year and still give generously of heart and mind to all of them; but a woman's health must be the guide.

I am a young wife and mother who would appreciate some advice. My husband is from a very fine family who have always had the better things of life. I, on the other hand, haven't a very good education. It was quite a struggle for my parents to send me to high school and one year of college. My husband and I love each other very much and his sister and parents treat me as if I were really one of the family. But I fear the day will come when, if I don't know how to carry on a conversation about something other than the daily news and the baby's newest tricks, I shall be left out. Could you help me by telling me what books I can read? I have three or four hours a

day which I can devote to reading and study, and want
so badly to learn. I feel it is necessary for my husband to
have a wife who can carry on an intelligent conversation
with his clients and our friends.

My dear, education is not entirely a question of what you learn in school or college. It is largely a question of the opportunities you have to talk with intelligent people and to become acquainted with as many facets of life as possible. One cannot give you a list of books which in themselves will make you a person of culture. To have read some, at least, of the classics is valuable to anyone. You can get good translations of some of the old Greek philosophers and old Greek plays. You can read some history, books about art, modern philosophers, biographies of famous men; and, of course, some of the best-known fiction writers in American and English literature, such as Dickens, Scott, Hawthorne, and so on, as well as poets and modern writers, all add to your background.

The field of learning is so wide that none of us can ever say we know much; and perhaps if you find one or two things that interest you, you might read a little more deeply along those particular lines and, above all, think about anything you read so you will have something to contribute that is the expression of your own character and personality. It is what you sift through your own mind and think about which makes you a more interesting person and therefore better able to interest other people.

My future father-in-law has given my bride-to-be and
myself the choice of a big wedding or a cash payment of

$2,000, *which he says is about what the wedding would cost. We badly need cash—it could be the down payment on a home—but my bride has chosen the big wedding. Mrs. Roosevelt, do you think you could possibly make such a choice under the circumstances?*

My dear young man, you and your bride-to-be must discuss this question together. No outsider should interfere in anything so personal. If you need the $2,000 for a down payment on a house, you and she should talk it over. It may be that she wants this day to remain with her as a wonderful day and hasn't given much thought to the future and the need to own a home.

Among my young, newly married friends there seems to be general agreement that women must do about 90 per cent of the adjusting in marriage. Do you think this is true? Do you think it is fair?

I do not know about the percentage. I do know that both parties to a successful marriage have to do a good deal of adjusting, and as women are usually more adaptable, I should not be surprised if they did the adjusting a little more gracefully and successfully than men. Anything is fair which brings you and your family success and happiness.

5. on In-Laws

Do you think that the saying is true, "A son is a son until he gets a wife, but a daughter is a daughter all her life"? Most people, I find, do; but I think a son can never be as close to a mother as a daughter. I don't feel his marriage has anything to do with it.

I think this is a question of individuals entirely. I have known many sons who were devoted to their parents and who remained close and as devoted after they were married as they had been before. Naturally a man has to give more time to supporting and living with his family when he has one, and he will not be quite as free, perhaps, to be with his parents, but closeness does not imply constant association. A daughter when she is married is in exactly the same position as a son: she has a family of her own which she has to look after; but again I have known many daughters to stay close to their parents.

The real answer, of course, is the quality of the relationship that exists between parents and children, and it may exist with either a son or a daughter, or it may exist with both sons and daughters in a family, and marriage does not have to change it.

My husband and I support his mother. She has reached the age where she can no longer live entirely alone, so we built an apartment onto our home for her. We cut a door between the two apartments, which was to be used as a passageway only. I have an exacting job, and when I get home I need rest and privacy. However, my mother-in-law seems to feel it unjust that I wish the door closed. Am I being silly about this?

I think you are very wise to keep the door shut between your mother-in-law's apartment and your own house. It is a great mistake, even when you love someone very much and he is very close to you, not to be able to close a door when necessary. If you have a job you must insist that your life is your own, to be lived with your husband and not in constant contact with anyone outside. To have a door between your house and your mother-in-law's apartment is a great convenience and also must give her a sense of safety, but that is all it should do. It should not be constantly open so that you have no sense of privacy.

My first marriage ended very unhappily in divorce. A few years ago I met a man I thought I loved, but I was afraid to marry him for fear of repeating the first experience. We decided to live together for a while and see how things worked out. We are now happily married, but my family recently found out about our living together and won't have anything to do with us. Do you think their attitude is fair?

You are putting a difficult question up to me. Your family has, of course, a right to act as they see fit. However, it is my experience that whatever families may do temporarily, there is no way of dissolving the family tie. Your children remain your children, your brothers and sisters remain your brothers and sisters. You may not approve of one another, you may at times almost dislike one another, but there is no real happiness in breaking family ties. It is better, I think, to accept whatever comes and give and keep the love which should exist among people of the same family.

Is there any way I can make myself a real unit in my husband's family? Four years ago we were married after a two-years' courtship and one-year's acquaintance with my husband's parents. They heartily approved our marriage, but now seem to want to antagonize. My husband says his mother tells him to "assert his authority as a husband over me" and "make me join his church." How should I meet such situations? I think families should be happy together and strongly united, but it breaks a girl's heart to know someone is trying to come between her and her husband. What can I do?

It is very difficult to answer your questions because there are so many contributing factors. Religious differences are always difficult, and if it is possible for you to join your husband's church, I would certainly do so. Of course I realize there may be some fundamental differences in belief, which make that impossible. In which case, I would try as far as possible not to argue about the situation.

Former generations thought much more about the word "obey" in the marriage service than we do today, and it may be that your mother-in-law is jealous if your husband is happy with you and forgets to write to her, or leaves too much of the contact between his mother and his own family to be made by you. Husbands have a way of doing that, and unless a mother is unselfish and understanding, it is very hard for her to take. Be patient and try not to make a break—then I think it will work out.

I am a woman of thirty-five with a husband and three children. My problem is that my recently widowed mother feels that I am obligated to take her into our home now that she is alone. Financially, we are able to provide her with an apartment of her own, near enough to us for friendly visits, but enabling us to keep our privacy as a family. Don't you think this is better than having three generations under one roof?

I have always believed that we older people are better off when we live alone, much as we long to have our children with us and much as we love them. We are usually not good for our children or for their children when we live with them. It was a very wise provision of nature's to give people their children to bring up while they are young. Older people can help from experience, but sometimes they have had too many experiences to make it wise for them always to be around the young.

My husband's mother is coming to live with us. She has lived by herself far away for a long time and has been extremely unhappy and lonely. We have had an unusually happy marriage and I have a happy disposition, but when she's here I find it is all I can do to keep from displaying ill temper and being depressed. She and my husband seem so happy together and I feel like a wet blanket and finally lose confidence in myself. My husband is a fine man with a strong character. I have three lovely sons—one a small baby. I want to do a good job in bringing up our children. How can I learn to relax and to have positive thinking about this? Is there anything I can read that will help?

If I were you, I would have a talk with your mother-in-law and with your husband, together or separately, as you find easier, but I would tell them both the same things: namely, that somehow a way must be found in which you can be included in the pleasures they find in their mutual companionship. You must, of course, make an effort to be companionable. If your mother-in-law is going to live with you, definite rules as regards the children should be decided on. You must have the final say-so, and there must be no effort to sabotage your discipline or your position with the children. Grandmothers can be a great help, but they can also be a heart-rending burden to their daughters-in-law, and only honesty between all concerned can save that situation. Honestly talking over things and not repressing your feelings, but making an effort to be kind and spontaneous in your contacts, will, I hope, bring you success.

I have been married for almost a year, and during that time have known very great happiness. I love my husband dearly, and have every reason to believe he feels the same way about me. I think he is a model husband— kind, considerate and loving. There is only one area of our lives where we have ever had any disagreement or unpleasantness. Even before our marriage, my mother-in-law and I came into a conflict of minds which has not improved with time. Although I am not happy about this lack of friendliness between us, it is my husband's attitude which makes me most unhappy. In every disagreement between his mother and myself I have never known him to defend me, my ideas, actions or points of view. Rather, he nullifies every effort of mine to explain my point of view by an effort at nonchalance and an apologetic attempt to soothe his mother's ruffled feelings. I cannot understand why he should refuse to defend me even when I am right, nor why he is emotionally tied to his mother, unless it is a subconscious feeling of obligation. She is both poor and a widow. What would you advise me to do about this situation?

I would advise you to try to refrain from putting your husband in a position where he has to take sides between you and his mother. It is hard for a man to side against his mother even if he feels his wife is right, and I think you will find that if you just keep quiet, he will gradually come to take up the cudgels in your behalf. Of course, if your mother-in-law lives with you, I realize that that is an extremely difficult situation because the rubs and disagreements must be very constant. If it is possible it would be better if you could at least live in separate quarters. I think you would find it easier to get along.

My boys are married and live not far from us in the same city, yet there are weeks at a time when I do not see them or talk to them unless I call them up. I'm certain they love me and yet they are unconsciously negligent. I don't want to put it on a "duty" basis and I try every way to be the kind of mother a married man wants. What do you advise?

If I were you, when I wanted to talk to my boys or their wives, I would call them on the telephone and I would try to make some kind of regular weekly arrangement with them. Perhaps you could have lunch or supper together on Sundays, but do not make them feel that they can never break the engagement. Sometimes it is easier to do something that you can count on and know is going to happen, which will bring you together and keep the family spirit alive.

The young people are busy and have many interests of their own and it is harder for them to find the time to call you than it is for you to call them. I would not do it too often, but once or twice a week would show you are interested and want to keep in touch.

Do you think a mother should accept her son's foreign wife and child even though he was engaged to a lovely American girl? There are thousands of the girls overseas, deliberately roping these boys in. Our Government seems to be more concerned over other countries than our own people.

I do not see what the Government has to do with our

acceptance of the wives whom our sons marry. Unfortunately, being engaged to someone is not quite the same as being married. If a young man marries someone else, the girl to whom he was engaged has no redress, but if the young man marries and leaves his wife, the situation is, of course, different. Therefore, I think whether the young man who married during his service abroad was engaged or not, a mother will have to accept the girl to whom her son is married. If there are children from the marriage, we most certainly will want to get on, since the children are our own blood. Paternity is something which cannot be wiped out. If we are wise I think we will learn to love the women our sons marry.

We will remember that the wives gave our sons, in the days that were hard, love and affection and a cure for the loneliness which might have been unbearable.

It is true that there are some foreign women who have "roped in" our young men and married them for selfish reasons, but I hope they are in the minority.

The best safeguard any boy could have, of course, was the knowledge that he had the love of his people at home, waiting for him to return, and their constant attention as far as the war would allow, during the time he was overseas.

Young people are prone to fall in love through propinquity. If they have married, we will be wise to do all we possibly can to help them in this new adventure, since we desire their happiness above all else in the world.

My husband and I do not agree on an important matter. I think we should help our daughter while her ex-

serviceman husband is attending college. They have some
help from the Government and his folks have been con-
tributing each month. Our incomes are about the same.
Do you think that the boy's folks should stand all of the
expense just because the man is supposed to be the bread-
winner? The young couple have a small child so my
daughter is unable to help her husband make a living.

I think perhaps your husband is right in feeling that the
boy and his parents would prefer not to have you give
stated sums of money toward the support of your daughter. They certainly would not object to your giving presents now and then, as you are able, either small sums of
money for specific things the young couple need, or some
things for the baby. That would not hurt the boy's feelings or make him feel he was less the breadwinner and
responsible for his family.

Although I am 19, I look only about 16. Maybe this is
why my parents have always treated me like such a baby.
I was never allowed to go out with boys until I was a
senior in high school. I was married shortly after I gradu-
ated and am going to have a child soon. We have been
married almost a year and have never had a real fight.
I am happier than I have ever been. My problem is that
my parents never have approved our marriage and seem
to resent my husband. How can I help to change this?

I do not like to give advice in such intimate family matters as these, where the feelings of the individuals involved enter into the solution.

In a general way, however, I should say that it might
be that your parents found it hard to adjust to having a
child, whom they had always regarded as a baby, actu-

ally living a life of her own and belonging primarily to her husband. If that is the cause, it will take time and patience both on your part and on your husband's part, and an effort on the part of your parents, to realize that all people grow up and that parents often have to develop interests of their own when their children leave them.

I have read that you were such a splendid wife because you were trained by your mother-in-law. This is an old European custom. Why don't more American mothers of sons give the new bride or bride-to-be a few pointers on how to be a good wife? Don't you think that if this custom were more generally observed there would be fewer divorces?

I do not know where you read that my mother-in-law trained me. I think I said she taught me a good deal about housekeeping and her own way of doing things. I do not know that I was a very good wife. One can only do one's best. I do not believe anybody, no matter how wise, can teach another woman to be a good wife. I am afraid the older generation can rarely give advice to the younger. I think training from a mother-in-law would result in more divorces rather than fewer.

6. on Children

A *neighbor of mine who reads child-psychology books
says I shouldn't spank my children or raise my voice when
they're bad. Would you be kind enough to tell me how
you punished your children when they misbehaved?*

I tried never to punish any of my children while I was
angry, and I do not think I ever raised my voice. When
they were very small I took them, on a number of occasions, to their father at the end of the day and asked
him to spank them. I knew they would receive a mild
spanking! I would never spank a child who is old enough
to be reasoned with, because I think it does hurt his
sense of self-respect.

There are many other ways in which children can be
punished. They can have things they like taken away
from them, and they can be deprived of certain privileges. Above all, they can feel the displeasure of the people they love. That, I have always found, is the worst
punishment one can administer.

*My five-and-a-half-year-old son asked me, "Mother, what
makes war?" I don't know what to say. How can you answer a small boy like this in terms he'll understand?*

I think the only thing to do is to explain to him that nations are not very different from individual people. He
knows there are times when he quarrels with his play-
mates. Make him analyze what brings about those quarrels and he will soon understand how, on the national
level, wars occur in the world.

*Did you let your children read the funnypapers when
they were young?*

I never found it a question of keeping my children from
reading or allowing them to read the funnypapers. They
just naturally do it. There were not so many comics
when my children were young, but I feel quite sure I
would have let them read them if there had been more.

*Did you use a book on child psychology for bringing up
your children? Which one?*

I had Dr. Holt's baby book, which was considered the
best at the time, and I followed that very carefully in
the physical care; but in the days when my children were
babies there was much less knowledge of psychiatry and
psychology, and I fear they suffered from lack of knowledge on the part of their parents in this important side
of a child's upbringing.

*How old were your children when they stopped believing
in Santa Claus? What did you tell them at the time?*

I do not remember the exact age when my children
stopped believing in Santa Claus. What I told them

was that of course there was a Santa Claus. He might not actually come down the chimney, nor perhaps have a sleigh drawn by reindeer, but I explained that in every home where the parents tried to give their children a happy time at this season of the year there was a Santa Claus. The old stories and legends were to be read and enjoyed and, if possible, preserved because they told of the different ideas and customs that had existed in many parts of the world.

What books did you read your children when they were little? There's so much trash on the market today, I simply don't know how to choose. My little boy is seven, and my girl is three.

We read a great many books to our children when they were small, beginning with *Peter Rabbit* and going on through Shakespeare's plays, *Ivanhoe*, *The Old Curiosity Shop* and many of Kipling's and Stevenson's stories. For the three-year-old I should think some of the picture books on farms and trains and the like would be both stimulating and interesting. For the seven-year-old I should think you might subscribe to a children's book club. In this way you will get a good assortment of books that will begin to give the child an interest in owning his own library.

Did you or your husband ever help your children with their homework?

Yes, both of us did. My husband was better at mathematics than I was, so he dealt with all the problems of that kind, but it seems to me that I have listened to end-

less words being spelled, and answered questions on almost all subjects.

Our youngest boy objects strongly to wearing hand-me-
down suits from his older brothers. I think he would feel
a little better about it if I could tell him that the sons
of the President of the United States also wore hand-me-
downs. Is this true?

Of course it is true in any large family where there are
several boys. We passed on clothes from the older children to the younger ones as they were outgrown before
they were worn out. Tell your boy it is too bad to be
born after the others but that is one of the things that
many children have to endure.

My sister died recently, leaving her nine-year-old daugh-
ter in my care. I know you went through something like
this yourself as a child, and thought you might suggest
ways my husband and I could make this little girl happy.
And mistakes we might avoid.

The great thing, I think, is to make children feel that
they are needed and actually belong in the family. Give
them certain responsibilities, and they will respond with
confidence and joy. If this child is sensitive, avoid talking about her before other people and letting her over-
hear your remarks about what you are doing for her. The
main thing is to love her and let her give you her love.

How did you break your children of thumbsucking when
they were small?

Not all of my children sucked their thumbs, though I

remember having trouble with two of them. In those days we put the hands into Celluloid balls at bedtime. I do not know whether this was a mistake or not. I am now told that thumbsucking should be permitted. Many ideas change as the years go on.

How old do you think a child should be before he gets a dog of his own?

A child should not have a dog of his own until he or she is able to take care of it, dependable enough to attend to the dog's wants daily without being told and has enough common sense not to hurt the dog or be unkind to it out of thoughtlessness.

When you have warned your children that such-and-such proposed actions would be bad for them—would bring them pain, or unhappiness, or hurt feelings—and when they went stubbornly ahead and met setbacks, and came to you for consolation, could you always keep yourself from saying, "I told you so!"?

I do not remember ever having been so unwise as to say, "I told you so." I think I was usually so mindful of the many times when I had done exactly the same thing myself that I was not tempted to bring the question up. Besides, when those you love suffer, even though you may have tried to explain to them that it might happen, you cannot help feeling sad with them and not wanting to add to their pain.

Would you be willing to tell me how you handled jealousies among your children?

I can't remember that there were many jealousies. I

can remember Anna as a very little girl pushing her brother over, which we thought showed she was jealous. But it did not last long, and she got over it without any effort on our part. As the children grew older I do not remember their showing any signs of jealousy of each other.

We have adopted a baby. Do you think the good environment we plan to give him will make up for what may have been an unfortunate heredity?

The argument as to whether heredity or environment is more important in a child's final development has never been settled. Of course, it may well be that the child you have adopted may not be unfortunate as far as his heredity is concerned, unless you know something definite, in which case you should watch and try to counteract any harmful tendencies. It always seems to me that environment means more than heredity in the long run and that with knowledge one can work intelligently to counteract anything harmful in the child's heredity.

My twelve-year-old son is forever after his father to buy him a rifle. The whole idea terrifies me. Don't you think he's too young? What did you do when your boys asked to have guns?

I think when a boy wants a gun it is not enough just to buy it for him. The father must teach his son how to use it and teach him the proper safeguards that must always be observed. If the boy does not observe them he should forfeit the gun for a certain length of time. Twelve years does not seem too young to be taught, and he may be a good shot. Many boys are at that age. The important thing isn't whether he has the gun but whether he has been taught to use it with care and discretion.

How can I reassure my children about the atom bomb? They've heard so much about it on the radio and at school, it seems to be an obsession with them.

You can only free children from fear by developing a philosophy yourself which is free from fear, and by explaining to the children that to live in fear is worse than actually to face the danger of extinction. If you can give them a trust in God, that is the one sure way of being able to meet all the uncertainties of existence.

7. on Adolescents

My daughter is young and pretty and talented, but she hasn't any beaux. Friends of ours with only daughters seem to have the same difficulty. I'm afraid of meddling and making matters worse. But I'd like her to have a more satisfactory social life. What can I do?

I should think the simple thing would be to make it possible for your daughter to bring her friends to the house in a simple and easy way, never trying to do too much for them but making the young people feel welcome. If girls come, eventually boys will come too, and if your daughter does work in some organization like a church organization or the Y she is sure, sooner or later, to meet and make friends with young men as well as with other girls.

I read how shy you were when you were young, and I know you are very tall, which sometimes makes one shy. How did you overcome timidity? How can I help my very

*tall daughter to live a happy life and not be ashamed
of her size?*

I think the best way to help your daughter to become
unselfconscious about being tall is to give her dancing
lessons, so that she feels she knows how to control her
body and so that she moves with ease and grace. Being
athletic will help her too.

There are many tall people in the world today, and
she ought soon to be able to forget her shyness if it is
because of her size. If she is shy because of other reasons
I can only suggest that you build in her an interest in
other people, and as she forgets herself in her interest in
others the shyness will disappear.

*I have two young sons just entering adolescence. My hus-
band thinks I should explain the facts of sexual maturity
to them, and I think he should. We'd be interested to
know how you and your husband handled this problem.*

I think in the case of boys it is usually far better if their
father is able to explain such things as they need to
know and at the times when they need to know them. It
is so important to choose the right time, not to do it too
early and not leave it till too late.

My husband was extremely shy about discussing any
of these questions with our boys. I always answered
any question that was asked by any of my children
as truthfully as possible and told them what I thought
they were able to understand, and I never told them anything which was not true. I think probably some of the
masters in school were more helpful even than their fa-

ther with our boys, though he did agree that he would tell them what he felt was essential. I always had an idea that he told them comparatively little!

My teen-age boys are sowing their wild oats in a way that shocks me. When I remonstrate they say what's the use of being serious, they'll be in the Army soon anyway. What can I say to them?

I think you might say to your boys that if they are going into the Army it is a serious undertaking and sowing one's wild oats is no preparation. Going into the Army in peacetime is a great opportunity for training, and they should look upon it in that way. Going into the Army in wartime is a dedication to the preservation of a free world, and I personally would feel that with a background of good family life and a good education, they had an obligation to think through the very high purposes which they are serving and to try to help the other boys who will be serving with them to see that this is not the end of life but the real beginning.

What rules would you give us mothers for teen-agers who always want to watch TV?

I think, as in everything else, there must be some moderation in the time given to watching television. If there are special programs that teen-agers want to see, they should view them in their free time and not take time set aside for homework or some other more or less educational purpose. Many of my friends tell me that about an hour of television a day is all that they allow their teen-age youngsters.

At what age did you allow your boys to start smoking?

It really was not a question of "allowing" them. The school they attended did not permit them to smoke at school. They began to smoke in the holidays, when they were about seventeen years old. Both my husband and I used to suggest that moderation was a good thing, but we always preferred they be open about whatever they did, so smoking was never forbidden.

Do any of your children or grandchildren belong to sororities or fraternities? How do you feel about sororities?

I do not know whether any of my children or grandchildren belong to sororities or fraternities. At Harvard my boys belonged to various societies and clubs. I do not know much about sororities because I never went to school in the United States after I was fifteen, I never went to college, and my daughter was at Cornell only for a brief winter agricultural course.

I think fraternities and sororities are bound to bring a certain amount of unhappiness to young people, but if they do not breed discrimination and are just an effort to bring together young people of mutual interests regardless of race or religion, I do not know that they would be harmful.

My attractive sixteen-year-old daughter, a popular junior in high school, has been dating steadily. To this I have no objection, as she is a high honor student, but she repeatedly returns from dates on school nights well after midnight. Two or three years ago when she disobeyed, she went across my knee and was soundly spanked with a hairbrush. I think this practice should be utilized again.

My wife disagrees. I would like to know your views.

I am afraid, when you reach the age of sixteen, to be spanked as though you were eight or nine would be rather bad for your sense of dignity. At sixteen a girl should be reasonable enough so that you could talk over the question of hours which are kept during the school week. My daughter never allowed her very attractive, charming daughter to make any dates during the school week, and the youngster herself realized that it was a wise plan and never even asked to make them.

From the things I read and hear about teen-agers today
they sound like a crazy, irresponsible, insolent bunch.
Some people insist adolescents always act this way, but
I don't remember being that bad, do you?

I am afraid I cannot join the chorus that finds young people today crazy, irresponsible or insolent. I have nineteen grandchildren, and a number of them are in the teen-age bracket. They sometimes do things that show poor judgment, but the young people about me on the whole have good manners, are thoughtful of others and carry their responsibilities with remarkable efficiency.

I have always regretted that in my own teen-age I had so much responsibility that I never knew what it was to be carefree. It is in those years that one acquires a real *joie de vivre,* and it is a pity to miss out on it.

Did you have to cope with the awkward age in your
daughter? If so, how did you do it and keep the family
fur from flying? I have a daughter, sixteen, who wants to
wear her dresses too tight and too old, and wrong shades
of make-up. She also has a strange taste in friends and

*keeps too late hours. How can I avoid argument, yet in-
still in her some ideas of good behavior and good taste?*

Of course every youngster, boy or girl, goes through an
awkward stage, and family fur will fly, and you cannot
avoid arguments. I can remember very well periods when
my children felt very bitterly toward me, but we became
firm friends again as they grew older and realized there
was sense in what I made them do and in what I said.
The important thing is to love them and they soon
know you are not just trying to be disagreeable—which
they often think!

*Our pretty teen-age daughter wants as many clothes as
her friends have. My husband feels that she asks for
more than she needs. We can afford to buy them, but her
father says one evening dress is enough for any girl. I
want to know if he is right in denying her clothes that
we can afford. Should I insist that he give them to her?*

If your daughter is still of teen age, I should think the
need for clothes could depend largely on what you allow
her to do. If you allow her to go out a great deal in the
evening, she will get tired of wearing one dress, even if
you are clever about it and arrange it so that it can be
made to look differently. But if you are rather careful and
let her go out very little, which with teen-age girls would
seem wise, then I think her father is right and one evening dress with different accessories is enough. It isn't a
question of what one can afford these days. It is a question of what is the right and proper way to spend money.
The rule to be followed, it seems to me, is whether one
really needs things.

*We have to hide some of the magazines from our adoles-
cent children because of the references to liquor. What
can we do about it?*

    I cannot imagine why you should hide magazines from
your adolescent children because they have references
to liquor. Do you think your children can live in this
world and not know that liquor exists, or that the use
of it is condemned when it is used to excess, but that it is
a commodity on the market? I am afraid our adolescent
children are not dependent for their information on the
magazines which they find in their own homes, and the
effort to hide them will be of little use. I should be
inclined to tell them whatever you want them to know.
They have to live in the world, so you have to trust them
in the end.

*Do you think the young people of today are worse than
they were ten or twenty years ago?*

    Certainly not. I have lived more than sixty years and I
have heard young people condemned many times. I
think nearly every generation is better than the last, and
I certainly admire the present one.

8. on Education

{

The school board in my town refuses to raise teachers'
salaries. As a result, the best teachers have left. What can
I do to see that my children receive the best possible edu-
cation?

> I think you should try to get as many parents as you can
> find in your town to realize that teachers are more im-
> portant than anything except parents in the lives of
> children. If the majority comes to understand that, there
> will no longer be this stupid idea that money spent for
> good teachers is money wasted.

The overcrowded conditions of our public schools and
the low salaries of the teachers present a problem that
must be typical of our income group. Do you feel that it
is wise to make considerable sacrifice to maintain our
children in a good private school in order to get the
advantage of individual instruction that the public sys-
tem cannot give at this time? I hesitate to assume this

financial burden unless convinced that it is the wise
thing to do.

No, I have always felt that there was only one advantage in private schools and private colleges. That was if they were so conducted that they carried on the experiments in education which public schools and public colleges could not afford to do. Then private institutions of learning serve a good purpose.

On the whole, I think it more important that all of us send our children to public schools and try to make public schools, because of our interest, what they really ought to be. It is true that teachers' salaries should be higher, but only the acceptance of that fact by the taxpayers will ever bring it about. It is true that more money should go into education, but again it is the taxpayers' realization of this fact that will bring it about. I have always felt this way, but my mother-in-law felt very strongly about private schools and we deferred to her wishes where our children were concerned, but I am not at all sure that it was wise in all cases. I am quite convinced that it is not the right and public-spirited thing to do.

What is your opinion of the idea of teaching religion
in the public schools?

I do not think that religion can properly be taught in public schools. We decided long ago to separate church and state. The public schools, being financed and run by the states, should not teach religion to children. That should be the responsibility of the home and the church primarily, though it may be possible in certain cases to work out some form of spiritual expression which is acceptable to all the children in a school. I feel, however, this should never be forced upon any of them.

In some public schools they are making it compulsory for children to learn a foreign language in the early grades. How do you feel about this?

I am delighted to hear that this is being done. The earlier children learn a foreign language the easier it is. In the earlier years children learn almost everything by memory and by ear, and not by reasoning. Arithmetic, which calls for reasoning, is difficult for small children. Languages, if learned while children are young, are learned largely by ear, and not by grammar, and children get an accent better and find the language easier than if they wait until they are older. It is most important for our young people to learn languages now, since they are likely to work and be in countries all over the world. Making friends in foreign countries is easier if you know the language of the people you are with.

I am a teacher in a system that makes a big difference between salaries of men and women classroom instructors who have the same qualifications and experience. What is your opinion of such a practice?

I have long advocated equal pay for equal work. When a man has higher qualifications I think he is entitled to higher pay, but when the qualifications are equal I think teachers as well as all other workers generally should receive equal pay for equal work.

Don't you think that both education and racial discrimination could be helped by taking public education away

*from the states altogether and bringing it under the con-
trol of the Federal Government, so that it could be the
same all over the country?*

I think it would be a pity to take education away from
the states. I believe in Federal aid to states and in equal-
izing the opportunity for all children as quickly as it can
be done, but the smaller unit is important, since it
knows more about the teachers and children within the
state than the National Government. The National Government may well set standards below which no state
must fall. For instance, a certain number of school
weeks in a year, a certain rate of pay for teachers, a
certain standard of education where teachers are concerned, and so on; but to turn the entire control over to
the Federal Government would, I think, not be an improvement.

*As mayor of our small city, my husband has been ap-
proached by the National Committee for American Education to head an investigation into the textbooks, teaching staff, and so on, of our local school system to discover,
if any, and eradicate any subversive communist and socialist propaganda. What is your opinion of the National
Committee for American Education?*

As I understand it, this committee was set up to screen
textbooks and to look into teaching staffs to prevent the
teaching of subversive doctrines. My feeling about most
of the screening processes that are undertaken is that
they are a type of censorship and should be undertaken
only when very essential and that the people charged
with such a duty should be carefully chosen. I have an
instinctive feeling that censorship is bad, particularly

when it comes to censoring teachers. I think it may discourage any kind of liberal thought more often than it actually uncovers any communists. The communist is well enough trained to hide his opinions usually and to do his job in very indirect ways, but the liberal is apt to be forthright and inquiring and not always wary enough in hiding his intellectual explorations from those who label all inquiry as subversive.

Why should we screen out of our schools knowledge of either socialism or communism? Socialism is increasingly accepted in a number of governments in Europe and Asia, and though we have accepted only some socialist ideas, it would be very unwise if we did not learn about them and weigh our own system and its results against these other systems. It is only by greater knowledge and conviction and enthusiasm that democracy can be made to meet the needs of the people. Our economic system has to be modified from time to time to meet new needs, and certainly our children should be trained to understand and to analyze and to compare all that we do with other systems and other results throughout the world. Academic freedom is something we cannot afford to endanger. There is a difference between studying something to know and understand and refute that which is false, and inculcating a particular line for the purpose of making a convert. That is really where the line should be drawn, and no one should be prevented from spreading knowledge among young or old on any legitimate subject. Calling anyone with a liberal or inquiring mind a communist or subversive person is a dangerous habit which has shown a tendency to increase in the United States of late.

Do you agree with Dr. Bernard Iddings Bell, who says
in his book Crisis in Education *that today's schools are*
turning out "confused juveniles instead of educated
adults"?

That is the kind of generality which is extremely hard
to prove. Of course you will find some "confused juveniles" who have been through college, but you will
also find some "educated adults."

When people make such sweeping statements I think
they do very little good, particularly when they rarely
give a formula by which education can be made to produce mature and educated human beings able to be
useful citizens under a democratic system of government in a very troubled world. We are in an experi-
mental period at present, and I think all great institutions of learning are making experiments—some good
and some not so good—but sweeping generalities
will not help very much to improve our educational
methods.

What steps can individual parents take to raise teaching
standards and modernize school curricula in their com-
munity?

Parents can work to have higher salaries paid to teachers
so that teachers may be given better training and an
opportunity to take advantage of continuing educational
opportunities. It is essential that a teacher should have,
during her holiday period, a certain amount of travel or
further opportunity to study. Something should be done
to make it possible for him or her not only to have a
period of rest and leisure but to continue intellectual
growth, since any teacher gives out so much that she

must have a period in which she renews her strength and interests.

There will always be different opinions as to different methods of teaching, since new experiments must be tried out. If parents take real interest in finding out what is needed to give their children the maximum opportunities in different fields, however, they will be able to help obtain the kind of education that is needed in the modern world.

Did you or any member of your family get especially high marks in school? I don't think marks mean much, and I'm in favor of abolishing report cards. Do you agree?

It happens that while I was in school in England, from the time I was fifteen until I was eighteen, I did get fairly high marks. My husband got high marks in the things in which he was interested. My brother too had exceptionally good grades in both school and college. My children had high marks when they were interested and really wanted to work, but otherwise they just "got by," which always used to make me very angry.

I do not think I should want to abolish report cards. I might want to abolish marks of certain types, because I think it is hard to make them accurate; but report cards in general, I think, give an idea of the effort and the amount of work done, thus enabling the parents to keep in touch with what the child is doing and co-operate with the school.

In our freshman year at high school we had a course given by a public-health nurse covering many phases of health, and also some sex education. We liked it because it was

*the most wholesome and natural approach and we could
ask questions which we hesitate to discuss with our parents. But the course was so short! Why can't all high
schools have a semester of this kind of instruction, just
when girls need it most?*

> If such a course is well given, I think the kind of instruc-
> tion that you seem to have had is well worth while; but
> if it cannot be given well at school, then I think the
> parents should manage to answer the questions and a
> child should not hesitate to ask whatever is on his or her
> mind. This is natural curiosity, and knowledge is neces-
> sary for safety.

*Many people have not had the opportunity to advance
their formal education as they would like. What books
or other reading material would you suggest to one who
would broaden his views of today's problems as well as
learn facts of the past? What qualities go to make a "refined person"?*

> I am afraid my list of books, since I have never under-
> taken to make up a "five-foot shelf," or anything of the
> kind, would be a pretty long list, because there are
> many things in history and biography and science and
> fiction that one would not like to feel one had never at
> least dipped into. I think people must follow their own
> desires and find out what interests them and take every
> opportunity to read whatever comes their way in order
> to find out if they can develop new interests in sub-
> jects which they never happen to have come in contact
> with before. It is well worth while to belong to a li-
> brary and go to the library and browse through the
> books and see what one becomes interested in.

I am not able to define that particular word "refined." I suppose it would require good taste to be a refined person, but I do not think I want to be refined. There is a certain lack of vitality in the word. I want to be informed, intelligent and ever curious. That would seem to me a more interesting approach to life than the effort to become a refined person.

What ten books should one read before considering oneself well educated?

I am afraid there are no ten books which will educate anyone. Education is not merely a question of reading ten books. You might get from a library a list of ten books that everyone should read, but that would not mean that because you read them you were educated. Education goes on all the days of our lives and is acquired not only in school but in actual living.

If you were sending a daughter away to college today, would you rather she went to a women's college or a coeducational university?

I think on the whole I would prefer a women's college, because there is less distraction for the studies we hope the girl is going to pursue—although that depends on the girl, of course. For some, however, it would be far preferable to be thrown in daily contact with boys. Therefore, I would leave this to the individual parents and the girl in question.

I am seventeen years old and have just finished high school. My mother insists that I go on to college, but I would rather take a job on the newspaper at home.

Mother says I will always regret missing college, but it seems to me the women I admire most in public life never went to college. Don't you think the world is better training for a newspaperwoman than the classroom?

I am afraid I do not agree with you. There are certain kinds of knowledge acquired in the classroom—history, grammar, a knowledge of literature—which, if you want to be a really good newspaperwoman, will be invaluable to your career.

My husband always complained bitterly that even some of the best newspapermen lacked sufficient knowledge of certain countries when he visited them and that he was constantly briefing them on trips to give them more background which would make their stories more interesting and understandable.

I know it is hard, when you want to take a job, to stick to the kind of work college means when you are not going to college just to enjoy yourself. But if you are serious in making newspaper work your career, you had better get as good a background and training as you possibly can.

Neither my husband nor I went to college and have often been sorry. Our seventeen-year-old daughter has taken the college preparatory course at school, but has no interest in going to college. She graduated this spring and is entered in one of the well-known women's colleges. Although it means financial sacrifice to give her a college education, we feel it is money well spent. While our daughter is willing to abide by our wishes, are we correct in forcing her to do something she hasn't the slightest desire to do just because we know the advantages?

I doubt very much whether your daughter would profit by going to college if she really does not want to go. Why don't you let her work for a year? Then she might find out what she wants to do in life and what advantages college might have for the particular thing she is interested in. Many girls who marry and run a home and never expect to hold a job or have a career find that college training would have been invaluable in the home. Until she finds it out, however, and really knows how she wants to use these years in college, it seems as though you would be making a sacrifice and your daughter might get very little out of it.

9. on Self-Help

---

*Were you honestly as timid as your son Elliott pictured
you in a recent article? If so, how did you get over it?*

Yes, I was just as timid as Elliott said I was. I got over
it because I had to get over it! My husband took it for
granted I could meet any situation, and little by little
I found I could, and I became so interested in what I
was doing I forgot myself and my own fears completely.

*Do you manage to set aside any time each day so you
can be by yourself and meditate?*

Yes, at night.

*Please tell me what you think makes a good speaker,
and to what do you attribute your success as a public
speaker?*

I do not know that I have been particularly successful
as a public speaker. I think I have made progress. I
found I did not know how to control my voice, so I took

some lessons to help me to do so. Then I worked very hard to think out the things that I wished to say and to find ways in which I could hold the attention of an audience. If I were to define what I believe makes a good speaker, I should say:

a. It is essential to be heard.

b. A speaker must have something to say.

The way it is said and the effectiveness of the presentation are largely something that has to be developed through practice.

I would be grateful to know how you conquered your fear of learning to swim, as I myself have terrible fears about it.

I had to teach my two youngest boys to swim, since their father was ill, so I took a course at the Y.W.C.A. and just made myself put my head under the water.

You wrote that you attribute your great energy to the fact that many years ago you learned how to relax and to be disciplined. What, exactly, do you mean by "disciplined"—allowing yourself to feel only constructive emotions, or what? And how do you learn to relax?

Physically I think the simplest way to relax is to lie flat on the floor or on a bed without a pillow, with one's arms at one's sides and one's ankles crossed, and then sink into the floor or the bed, letting go so completely that anyone can pick up a leg or an arm and it will just drop back without any effort on your part to prevent it. At the same time you must think of something so monotonous that it is practically like keeping your brain from working actively. You will find that fifteen minutes of rest in this way will be equivalent to a much longer period in which you toss about and think of the things which may have worried you.

Discipline is a bit more difficult to describe. I think it is the quality which makes you realize that things which happen in life have to be accepted and faced, that there is no use in kicking against the pricks. If you have done your best you can do no more, and so you are at peace with yourself and your surroundings. The person who hasn't learned emotional control when he is young will find it harder and harder as he grows older to control his nerves and his emotions. This is an important part of a child's training, but of course life teaches people who haven't acquired it when they are young and most of them have to acquire it later on. That is much harder and means greater suffering to the individual. Probably the thing to learn is to face yourself honestly in relation to other people and to the situations in which you find yourself.

How did you learn to speak French so well? And what is the best way, do you think, to learn a language, outside of living in the country itself?

My mother had a conviction that it was essential to study languages, so when I was a baby she had a French nurse for me, and I spoke French before I spoke English. My mother insisted that there should always be in the house a French-speaking person, and I also took lessons from a very good French teacher and spent three years in a French school in England, where we had to speak French exclusively.

The only ways I know of to learn to speak a foreign

language are either to live in a foreign country or to be as much as possible with natives of that country and speak the language as frequently as possible. It helps to read a great deal in the language, and it is desirable to read aloud.

How much sleep do you average a night? How much do you feel you need for a typical busy day?

I am afraid I vary the amount of sleep which I get. There will be nights when I get only four or five hours of sleep, but then I try to make up by a good eight-hour night's sleep every week or so.

Have you ever dieted to lose weight? If so, could you tell me the basis of the diet?

Yes. I ate as little as possible, but enough fruit and vegetables to keep well. No bread or potatoes or sweets, and no alcoholic or soft drinks.

In a magazine article I read that you have trained yourself so that you can take short naps when you have a little free time during the day. I have heard of other people being able to do this. Are there any words of instruction or advice that you could give to help another person develop this ability?

I would only suggest that you be so tired that you cannot keep your eyes open. If you are as weary as that and have learned to relax instead of becoming keyed up and tense, you will find that your eyes will close and you will be asleep for a few minutes until some unexpected sound awakens you. It may be for one or three or five minutes, but the principal requirement is that you be very weary, and still able to relax. Don't do it in an automobile, however, unless you pull off the road first!

How do you "let off steam" when you are in a good healthy rage?

I cannot say that I ever really allow myself to be in a good healthy rage! If something annoys me very much my children tell me I become extremely quiet, and it used to be a byword in the family: "Look out, ma's very quiet." I think probably the life I have been obliged to lead has disciplined me more than is either wise or necessary for most people. Ordinarily I would say a good way to let off steam is to exercise hard.

I need to discipline my speech and don't know exactly how to go about it. I often say something quite innocently that offends the person with whom I am talking. For instance, I mentioned someone's being fat to a fat lady. My face was as red as hers when I realized what I had done. I am thirty-nine years old and feel that I should have been able to overcome this fault long ago. What would you suggest?

I haven't any idea, my dear lady. Many of us say thoughtless things, but if they are not meant unkindly they will not be taken seriously by those to whom they are said. I think the only thing you can do is to practice thoughtfulness, and then perhaps you will speak more slowly and think first. As a matter of fact, it is really impossible never to say things which come naturally into the conversation, even if they do seem to allude to some individual in the group.

I have terrible attacks of stage fright every time I have to make a speech or preside over a meeting. Can you suggest any way to cope with this?

Stage fright is something you can overcome by constant practice. One good way to help yourself through the first crucial moments is to write out the beginning and the end of your speech or statement, perhaps only a paragraph. Then you know you have something before you to hold on to if you are frightened so much you are at a loss as to how to begin and then become wound up and do not know how to stop! If you try this method of writing out the beginning and end and carefully thinking out the points you wish to make during your speech—or, if you preside over a meeting, the particular points you want the meeting to keep in mind so that the objective of the meeting is always in sight—I think you will find your stage fright will grow less and you will be able to preside or make your speech without too much difficulty.

How do you keep from worrying? You must have many more worries than most of us, yet worry never seems to get you down.

Everyone living, of course, has worries; and if they have many people whom they care about, naturally they are concerned about them and their worries. But I learned many years ago that worry which did not lead to being able to do something was useless. The best way to alleviate worry is to do all you can.

10. on Women

What do you consider the best years of a woman's life?

I do not really know what are the best years of a woman's life, because it depends so much on how she develops. If she is able to learn from life to get the best out of it at all times, then probably at whatever age she is those years will be the best she has had. But we do not all do that.

If you ask me what years I thought were the most enjoyable I would again have to qualify my answer because the enjoyment is different at different times. Certainly the years when women have young children are very rewarding, but again they are often filled with anxiety.

The years of youth, when there is less responsibility, are enjoyable—but the anxieties of youth are also very marked, and there are few young people who escape them.

The best thing we all can do is to learn to make use of

the years as they go by and enjoy whatever period of life we are in.

Do you think it's such a tragedy for a woman not to marry?

That is a question that can only be answered by the individual women themselves. For some women it would be a very serious tragedy. For others, perhaps not a tragedy at all. Speaking generally, I think women who have had the experience of marriage are happier, and most women who have had no children regret the lack of this experience and feel at times that not having the companionship of a husband and children is a great loss.

Clubwomen take such a beating from the cartoonists and jokesters that I'm almost ashamed to admit that I am one. Do you think we bring this on ourselves?

Yes, very often. We are apt to behave unnaturally and a little pompously, and that is really what makes us a subject for the cartoonists.

I am a woman about forty years of age and not bad to look at, have a college education, a good responsible job, sense of humor, good disposition, and am not aggressive or set in my ways. I have never had the opportunity of meeting eligible, unmarried men and I am craving a home and companionship. I enjoy cooking and making others happy. Have you any suggestions?

Your situation does not sound to me very desperate. It seems to me that at your age it ought to be possible to make opportunities for meeting eligible unmarried men. Use a little ingenuity in your business to make friends. It is not impossible for a woman to do some entertaining on her own, and to issue some invitations if she becomes friendly with people whom she meets either in the course of her work or in the course of her outside activities.

Lately, everyone seems to be criticizing women for bad manners. Do you think women have worse manners than men?

I have never tried to compare the two, but I should think, on the whole, that women have better manners than men because good manners arise from thoughtfulness for others. The very nature of their job in life makes women think about others around them more than men usually have to do.

Like many women in their twenties, I am beginning to face and fear a future alone with no husband for love and companionship. What advice would you give those of us who do not marry, to permit us to lead full and happy lives, free of the fear of loneliness? Do you think overeducation which lifts a woman above the intellectual level of the people she meets is ill-advised?

I should advise any young woman who does not marry to take a deep interest in young people, so that she will have the same satisfaction with other children that she might have had with her own. I should also advise her to build up very warm friendships and cultivate her interest in some kind of work which will tie her down to obligations, so that she will never find time hanging heavily on her hands and feel that her existence is profitless.

There is no such thing, from my point of view, as overeducation, nor being above any people because of formal education that you might have been fortunate enough to acquire. Anyone with character and the opportunity can acquire a formal education, and many people who have not had a chance for book learning are wiser than those who have had. If education hasn't given you enough understanding so that you can get on with people around you and appreciate their quality, and perhaps help them through your opportunities to more opportunities of their own, so that their interests may coincide with yours, then I am afraid your education has done you more harm than good.

What, as you see it, is woman's function in society after middle age, when the years of childbearing are over?

If a woman is blessed with good health, she is freer after middle age to do things outside her home as her children grow up. If she has a home, however, and a husband to look after, and has been fortunate in having a number of children, she will find her freedom from family cares is purely a myth. They are different, but they are still fairly time-consuming.

Nevertheless, the most rewarding activity for any woman, young or old, is to meet the needs of those who are nearest and dearest to her. She will not meet these adequately, however, if she has no interests and occupations of her own, since it is important that young families should never have the feeling that the older members of the family are languishing for their constant companionship. This makes the time they spend together less enjoyable and makes a duty out of something which should be a pleasure.

What do you think is the reason so many European visitors get the impression that American women are not only bossy but do not even like men?

I did not know that this was an impression that many Europeans carried away with them after visiting this country, but it is a fact that American women cater less to their men than do the foreign women. I think there is more real equality here. Occasionally we find a spoiled woman among us, but that balances itself out, for occasionally we find a spoiled man. The kind of playing up to the men which is prevalent abroad, very largely because women are in the majority and men are in the minority, is not yet known in this country.

I am a widow of forty. While my husband was alive we were very happy. I loved him very much, but feel I am too young to spend the rest of my life alone. I am a working woman, so have an opportunity to meet new people every day. How much time do you think should elapse before I can decently be seen with other men?

Heavens above! You can decently be seen with other men whenever you feel like going out again. This is your life, not someone else's, and your own feeling is what is important, not what the rest of the world says. I never can understand why one cannot live one's life as one thinks is right. You can get rid of your neighbors, but you cannot get rid of yourself, so you are the person to be satisfied, not your neighbors.

*Many mothers "give up everything" for their children
and are then mortally hurt when children, in maturity,
feel that their mothers do not fit, in appearance or social
presentability, into their lives. Don't you think there is
a kind of "escapist selfishness" in this kind of mother
love that tries to live through the accomplishments of
their children what they could not or would not achieve
themselves?*

I think probably a certain amount of selfishness in all
mothers is good for children. We should realize that
children have to stand on their own feet and we should
not give up everything for them. The burdens in a
family should be mutually borne and children should
learn that they are a part of the community of the
family, and I do not believe that any mother does a wise
thing for her children when she makes life too easy for
them.

*As compared with men, what do you think are the chief
faults of American women, both as workers in organizations, in public, and as individuals? Are there any respects
in which as a group you think women are superior to
men?*

As workers in organizations I think sometimes women
are more sensitive to supposed slights and get their feelings hurt more easily than men. When you say "in
public," I suppose you mean in public office, and I
should say this same trait is visible there. They find it
hard to stand up under unfair criticism, and they are
easily discouraged.

As individuals I think you have a more difficult question because every woman is different just as every man

is different, and what you might say about one group even might not be true about another.

There is a large group of women, however, who lack self-confidence as individuals when they undertake anything outside of the traditional spheres in which women have always moved. Even as individuals the same sensitiveness to criticism is a drawback in family and social relationships. I think women are often superior to men in their intuition about people; in their executive ability when they are handling detailed work; and in their ability to subordinate themselves to a cause or to another individual if they think that is the way to serve a cause. You will laugh, ladies, but I think women often talk less and act more quickly than men.

*Since American women spend so much of their time in
business and politics, what can be done to keep them out
of the taverns? Do you think if taverns were licensed to
sell spiritous liquors only, and if tables and chairs for
women and soft drinks and all food and music were
banned in taverns, it would do any good?*
I haven't the faintest idea. Women nearly always go where men go. In the long run, it seems to me, the important thing is to make whatever place people go a decent place in which to be.

*Do you feel it worth while for a woman with children
to work if she can't earn at least $5,000 a year?*
No, I hardly think it would be worth while today for a woman to work and pay someone to take care of her children if she were earning less than $5,000 a year. She would want to get a very high type of person to be with

the children, and that would take so much of her salary it would not be worth while. However, many women have to work to support their children even if they are neglected, though Social Security and state mothers' pensions make this less frequent today than in years past.

Are you in favor of drafting women for defense work if we are involved in a full-scale war?

If we are involved in a full-scale war, I think every woman as well as every man should be drafted to do the work she is best capable of doing. A full-scale war at this time would mean such a complete change in all our lives that a draft of this kind would, I think, be essential. I hope, however, we will never have a full-scale war and that we, the human race, will have enough intelligence to avoid it, since from my point of view it would mean practically ending our civilization.

I dread the change of life. How did you keep it from interfering with your busy life?

It is largely a question of really being busy and keeping oneself interested. I know there are abnormal cases, but for the ordinary woman it is quite easy to carry on life in a perfectly normal and ordinary way. Discomforts are involved, but if you are busy and keep up your interests the discomforts will hardly be noticed.

11. *on Adversity*

We have just learned that our 12-year-old son will have
to wear braces on his legs for the rest of his life. We are
heartsick about this, and we hoped perhaps you could
tell us how we could make it easier for him.

I think you will find that at twelve your boy will make
his own adjustments. If he must wear braces he will
learn to get about and do it far better than you now
think is possible. I do not, of course, know what his
illness is, but it is possible that exercises might eventually strengthen some of his muscles. There are doctors
who make a specialty of this type of treatment.

If you knew that your children had been going through
periods of unhappiness and felt that they suffered be-
cause of mistakes in your previous upbringing of them,
how would you meet the thought? With what philoso-
phy would you accept your share of the blame for suffer-
ing you would like to wipe out or alleviate but were un-
able to? How should a mother meet such thoughts?

I rarely have known children who, at some time in life, did not feel that they were made unhappy because of the type of upbringing that they received. As children grow older, they often realize themselves that their home had nothing to do with the unhappiness that may come to them. Perhaps you brought them unhappiness by the effort to prepare them for life. All parents, I think, feel that they haven't always been wise and that they are in some way responsible if their children suffer later on because of traits of character which might have been obliterated when they were young. The only way I think that parents can meet this is to accept the fact that no human being is all-wise; no human being always lives up to the best that he is capable of, all the time. Failures come to all people. It is sad if they affect those whom we love, but all we can do is to be very humble and, as we gain wisdom, try to help all those who suffer and show our children where we made our mistakes.

We are coming to you for advice because we are ashamed to go to our pastor or anyone else we know. We found out recently through a note which we discovered in our seventeen-year-old son's pocket that he and his seventeen-year-old girl friend have had illicit relations with each other for more than two years. When confronted with the evidence they defiantly admitted everything. Our son wants permission to marry this girl as he says that he loves her. Her parents do not know about them. Should we tell them and have them help us decide what should be done? We truthfully told our boy the things which he should know through the years so he did not

*fall into temptation and yield through ignorance. He is
conscience-stricken about the whole affair but the girl
seems to be utterly devoid of a conscience.*

I think your son and the girl should go to her parents.
It is their story, not yours, that has to be told. Then you
and her parents could talk the situation over. It would
seem to me that if you are able to do so, you would want
your son to finish his education so as to be as well prepared as possible to take care of the girl he marries. Her
parents, I should think, would feel that they wanted her
to finish her education so that she would be well prepared to be a good wife.

In addition, two or three years may make a very great
difference in both of them and the fact that they had
to wait to marry until they were able to earn a living
would probably mean a happier future for them and
give them time to mature and realize that marriage is not
just a question of physical attraction but a life companionship into which many other things have to enter
if their lives are to be useful and happy together.

*Should an elderly woman with no means of livelihood
have a sense of guilt at having to take charity from the
county? True, I'm not physically fit to hold a job, and
my three daughters have all they can do to keep their own
families. But I can't help that feeling that if people knew
(besides the bank and county employees) I just couldn't
face them. Is it guilt or false pride? I earned my own
way since I was 13 years old, married at 17, widowed at
36, and lost close to $20,000 in the depression years.
Maybe it's that word "indigent" on the check. I don't
know. What do you think?*

I certainly do not think you should have any sense of guilt. In a few short years I hope Social Security will mean that everybody who has worked during the best years of their life will have sufficient to live on from the time they stop work. In the meantime, I wish that checks did not have to carry the word "indigent"; but just forget about it, and certainly do not feel any sense of shame or guilt.

How would you spend your time if you knew you had just six months to live?

I haven't the remotest idea. I think that situation has to be decided when you are obliged to face it. I rather think I'd try to go on living as usual, since that would be easier for others around me.

I am 60 and about to have my first operation. I know it's foolish to be frightened, but I can't help being. Have you ever had a major operation?

Yes, I had one once, and as I lay on the operating table I heard the doctor ask if I was gone, because my pulse was so low. But I came back quickly, and I have never again had anything like that happen, though I have had several minor operations since then.

My husband has cancer and doesn't know it. He begs me to tell him the truth about his sickness, but the doctor says I shouldn't. The situation is almost killing me. I don't know where to turn for advice. Can you help me?

No, I am afraid I cannot help you. The situation is a very difficult one for you, and I am deeply sympathetic, but only you and the doctor know your husband well enough to know whether the truth would make him face what lies before him or whether it would be better to let him go on without knowing. No outsider can make that decision for you.

Was your husband ever in great pain during his illness? What could you do to help him when this was the case?

Yes, my husband was in very great pain in the early months of his illness. There was nothing that could be done to help him except such things as the doctor ordered. The only other possibility was to try to provide him with as much entertainment as possible. I tried to get interesting books and have interesting people come to see him.

My husband has come back from Korea with both legs paralyzed. He is so depressed about his future. Can you tell me how I can help him? What comforted your husband right after his paralysis?

My husband always felt that if he worked hard he could improve his condition, and I think your husband should realize that he has even more chance to improve. My husband knew, too, that even if he was not actually improving in the strength of his legs he could learn to handle himself better, and the more he learned to be independent and to do things he had felt he might never do again, the more self-confident he became and the more cheerful he was about his illness. I think you will find with your husband that each victory will mean a great deal in his mental attitude.

My young son contracted infantile paralysis at the age of three. Now, eighteen months later, he is walking, aided by long braces and crutches. Because President Roosevelt rose so magnificently above his handicap, I would like to ask you what things meant most to him? What skills would you try to encourage if you were just starting someone off in life with that handicap?

First of all I think at your son's age you are apt to find that he will greatly improve as time goes on and may even recover entirely before he is grown. As far as my husband was concerned I think his most valuable asset was the tremendous number of interests which he had already acquired, so that even though he was condemned to sit still he was never condemned to mental boredom or inactivity. If he was not doing something with his stamp collection, he was poring over books, reading about the American Navy or about a period in history in which he was particularly interested, or he was building toy sailboats and using his hands, which seemed to give him a creative outlet. He often spent hours over catalogues adding to his various collections—stamps, naval prints, first editions, miniature children's books. Any number of things made the time spent in getting well a time in which there was opportunity to do many things that he ordinarily had not had time enough to do. Above all else, he had time to think. If you broaden your son's horizons and awaken his interest in as many things as possible you will find that it will help him all his life, no matter what degree of handicap he may have to endure.

My friend was killed in action overseas. This was two years ago, but he is still constantly on my mind. Nothing I can do nor anyone I meet seems to measure up to Bob.

*What is the best way to forget the past and look forward
to the future?*

> I know of no way to forget the past. Perhaps you can
> learn to live with it more happily, remembering what
> gave you joy, realizing that no one whom you loved and
> who loved you would want you to go on and lead a
> lonely life because you kept comparing him with the new
> friends that came into your life. You do not want to for-
> get Bob, but you do want to go on living happily, and
> perhaps you will love someone else just as much one of
> these days, but in an entirely different way.

*Can you recommend any book that will comfort a
woman whose husband died last year and whose only
son has just been killed in Korea?*

> I know of no other book but the Bible, in particular the
> Twenty-third Psalm, that I think might help. What a
> tragedy for a woman to go through! I hope she is able
> to work and that there is something she would be
> interested in doing. That would seem to me to be the
> one thing that may make life worth living to her again.

*A short time ago my husband died very suddenly. I feel
a great need for faith. But when I pray it seems to me
I am just mouthing words. I must find strength. Can
you tell me where you found it when your husband died?*

> I think if you keep on praying you will find that strength
> will finally come. Pray for strength to meet whatever
> situation you must meet in life, and the act of faith often
> produces remarkable results.

12. on Religion

Do you believe that Christianity has failed or that the United States is not really Christian but just a nation that gives lip service? Don't you think the United Churches is what is needed instead of the United Nations?

You put a great many questions into one, it seems to me, and each of them might well take a book to answer! Certainly, Christianity has not failed, but Christianity is something that is accepted or rejected by the individual, and even when he accepts it he may still not live up to it all the time or even part of the time. Nations are made up of individuals, but I do not think it would be fair to say that a nation has rejected Christianity because either among its citizens or in its government you found certain things which you did not think were compatible with your particular interpretation of the doctrines of Christianity.

Whether you believe as a Protestant or a Catholic,

or a Jew or a Moslem or a Buddhist, it is the fruits of your belief as evidenced in your daily life that are of concern to your fellow human beings. If you believe in God, you naturally think that as a Supreme Being He will not judge you by your conduct alone, but also, with His infinite knowledge, for your intentions, taking your temptations into account and sometimes giving you credit for your victories.

The United Nations is an instrument, a piece of machinery, through which human beings, imperfect as they are, strive for greater perfection. The churches on earth are in much the same position, only they supposedly strive for greater perfection only in the spiritual field, whereas the United Nations has to deal with both the spiritual and the material. We cannot do away with either; they have different functions, but the two functions complement each other and are valuable together.

It would help me in my church work if you would tell me your favorite verse or verses from the Bible.

My favorite verses are in First Corinthians, Chapter 13, which starts: "Though I speak with the tongues of men and of angels and have not charity, I am become as sounding brass, or a tinkling cymbal."

I have heard psychiatrists say that the Bible does not have adequate answers for man's problems today, and that it should be rewritten to eliminate confusion arising from outmoded theories. Do you think the Bible is out-of-date?

No, I do not think the Bible is out-of-date. It still seems

to me a remarkably wise book and very satisfying to read both as to form and content.

Has anything ever happened to you which made you believe in miracles? If so, would you mind telling me about it?

No, I am afraid nothing has happened to me which made me believe in miracles. I believe in the miracles reported in religious history, but I think some of them are to be interpreted more as parables than in exactly the way they are written.

Religion teaches us to live by the Ten Commandments and the Golden Rule. Yet this is impossible—and impractical if you have to work for a living. Don't you think we are kidding ourselves when we say we do live by them? Wouldn't it be more honest and better for us and the people with whom we come into contact if we worked out an ethical code which it would be possible to attain?

It is a very sad commentary on our society that many people would say as you do, that they cannot earn a living and really live with their neighbors according to the Golden Rule and the Ten Commandments. I have heard it many times, and recognize the fact that in order to keep a job you will sometimes have to make compromises. Make them as little as you can, and in your own life try to live in the way that you really feel you want to live. It will change even the business conditions under which you struggle at present. No ethical code will meet the situation any better than the old religious code. It is simply that not enough people have come together with the firm determination to really live the things which they say they believe.

Will you please state your views about immortality? Do you feel that we will see and know our loved ones again? I realize that this is a question which no one can answer positively, but you can help by stating your beliefs.

I really have never thought very much about immortality. I do not know whether I believe that the future produces people as they were here or not. I am not going to worry about it, because there is no way in which we can possibly know. It always seemed to me that it was incontrovertible that in some way there must be some kind of immortality, because it would be such a wasteful performance otherwise. I hope very much that in spirit the things that we cared for in people we will be conscious of again, but, after all, there is nothing we can do about the type of life that awaits us, and we waste our time when we speculate about it. This is one of the areas in which faith that whatever is in store will be for the good of mankind is about the best rock on which to build.

A preacher here in South Carolina told us you once said the Bible was just a bunch of fairy tales. I don't believe you said this, Mrs. Roosevelt, but would you mind telling me what you do think the Bible is?

I do not remember ever saying that the Bible was just a bunch of fairy tales. In fact, I know I never said it. I think I may have said that there are parts of the Old

Testament which as a child I was taught to take literally and now I assess some of these as having other than literal meanings. I think the Bible is one of the most valuable and beautiful books that was ever written, and I think the more we study it the more we understand and find new meanings in it. The New Testament, especially, seems to me inspired and easier for us to understand than the Old Testament. However, I find them both very rewarding reading, and, like many other people, I have found that to read even a few verses every day is a very helpful habit.

My wife, who is 65, cannot bear to have anyone mention
the subject of death. I think this is wrong, don't you?
Have you a philosophy about death that might help her?

Your wife may not want death mentioned because she is afraid it will make those around her sad, but I think death should be treated as naturally as one treats birth or any other great experience. The seasons merge into each other, the flowers die and are born again. We may not ever make up our minds as to exactly how the promise of immortality is carried out, but all of us have an instinctive belief in immortality. I have never understood why people worry about exactly what form immortality takes. We have to accept what is in store for us, so why worry about it? The incentive for us to live to the best of our ability every minute of our lives lies in this fact of immortality.

My husband says that he wants to be cremated when he
dies. I cannot bear the thought. It seems so unnatural.
Please tell me how you feel on the subject.

I cannot see why it seems unnatural, unless it is forbidden by one's religion. All of us eventually turn to dust and ashes, whether we are buried or cremated and have our ashes put wherever we specify. It looks to me as though it will become more and more difficult to find land for the cemeteries that are going to be needed by our increasing populations. In India people are burned on a funeral pyre, and I think cremation may well become a practice everywhere in the world. Personally I would feel it is quite a natural feeling on the part of your husband.

Should a wife raise a fuss because her husband refuses to include church support in the family budget? My husband and I are not churchgoers except at Christmas and Easter. However, both of our children were baptized in church and expect to be confirmed in church. I feel that obligates a family to help support the church. My husband doesn't agree. What do you think?

It all depends on whether one believes that a church is a good influence in the community. If one does, then as a good citizen, one has an obligation to support the church to which one belongs.

I belong to the Church of Christ and my husband to the Methodist. I want us to attend Sunday services together, but he doesn't feel that he can go with me, even though he promised to do so when we were married. I cannot go with him, because Christians of today are commanded to repent and be baptized, and there is no mention of a Methodist or any other church as far as I know in the entire New Testament. I feel that he should

let me take the two children with me because of the
promise he made. Do you agree with me?

I am a very poor person to answer this question. Denominations mean very little to me. I would go to any church available if I felt the need and it gave me help to live my life better. I think if we pattern our lives on the life of Christ we will find that He made little mention of denominations. He was a Jew and yet He founded the Christian religion.

I do not know the difference between the Church of Christ and the Methodists and, of course, you and your husband will have to decide between you what actually seems important to you, but to me the way your personal religion makes you live your life is the only thing that really matters.

Do you think it's possible to be a good Christian without
being a regular churchgoer?

Of course it is possible to be a good Christian without being a regular churchgoer. Nevertheless, going to church has two considerations in its favor. One is the personal satisfaction and benefit derived from the services; the other is the value of the example in the community which shows that a citizen is a Christian. There is value in showing publicly where one's allegiance lies.

13. on Prejudice

Did you ever say in any of your public utterances that you believed in racial intermarriage?

> I have no recollection of what I said on this subject, but it is quite obvious that racial intermarriage has been going on among many races on the face of the earth for many, many years, so my opinion for or against it would be completely useless.

At a meeting at which you were the principal speaker I overheard two women who appeared to be intelligent and leaders in their own communities state that they were not prejudiced, but they just "did not like Jewish people." How can we hope for lasting peace and better understanding among peoples of the world when here at home intolerance exists among people who are trying to assume positions of leadership?

> I do not think we can. Those of us who have prejudices will have to make every effort to overcome them, since

the only hope for peace in the world is to understand and like people of different religions and nationalities and races.

Last evening while conversing with some young women I have known for years, the subject of racial equality came up. To my dismay, several girls whom I had always considered fair and unprejudiced made such remarks as: "I don't believe in equal rights for colored and white people." Similar remarks were made regarding Jewish people. Will you kindly tell me how one goes about calmly trying to convince people who consider themselves "nice people" but harbor within their minds such prejudices? Every one of these girls is a member of some church in our community.

I would suggest that the girls you mention be given a copy of "In Henry's Back-yard" to read as a starter.

Sometimes I think we are a little too calm when we run up against this type of prejudice. However, the best thing to point out is that one is not asking for equal rights to begin with, but equal opportunities, and then when those are obtainable the rights will take care of themselves.

One might suggest that democracy is today at the crossroads, and unless we show some zeal in fighting for fundamental democratic beliefs, we may find other beliefs in the ascendancy.

We have found in a number of instances that states' rights had to be subordinated to the good of the whole people. When we flout the Constitution by an appeal to states' rights, we are, I think, courting disaster. Sooner or later a nation has to make up its mind to be a united

nation or fall apart, and the attitude of these young
ladies is an attitude which will bring about dissolution,
since we cannot remove people who have been here long
enough to become citizens.

My grandson says that the French attitude toward Ne-
groes is completely different from ours. Have you found
this to be true? If so, how do you explain it?

Your grandson is telling you the truth. There is no color
line in Paris, and a Negro is received exactly as a white
person. This is partly owing to the fact that for generations people from North Africa, India, Egypt and the
Near East, all of whom have dark skins, have been
frequent visitors and among these people there has been
intermarriage.

I am a citizen of Holland. Is it true, as people say here,
that colored people in America have a hard life? Is it true
that there are special places where they must live just like
the Indians? Do the Americans lynch a Negro when he is
trying to vote?

The colored people in America have in some ways a
hard life because they have been discriminated against
in many ways in the United States. They are not treated
as some Indians are, who are placed on reservations and
treated as wards of the Government. The Negroes are
full-fledged citizens, freed by Abraham Lincoln's Eman-
cipation Proclamation, but in large cities there are often
sections which become almost entirely occupied by different groups of people—colored people, Italian people,
Puerto Ricans, and so on.

Lynchings in the United States occur only very occasionally, and I do not think a lynching would occur in the majority of states because a Negro was trying to vote. It might in a few states be considered as a way to prevent the Negro from using the ballot.

What do you think of the statement of the Negro U.N. delegate, Mrs. Edith Sampson, that "millions of people throughout the world have not such brilliant living conditions as the Negroes of America."

I think Mrs. Sampson spoke with great knowledge and absolute truth.

I have an obviously Jewish name. My wife feels we should change it for the sake of our children. I am in a terrible state about this, not knowing if I should or shouldn't. I respect your judgment, Mrs. Roosevelt. Will you tell me what you think?

I would not trust my own judgment on this, so I asked one of my friends, who is a good American and has served in high positions in our government and whose name is unquestionably German-Jewish. He said he would certainly not change his name. That was my feeling, but I thought it only fair to ask someone who had been through circumstances similar to those which you and your wife and children are now facing.

Don't you feel that if the American Government spent half as much time solving the problems of its own minority groups as it does meddling in European affairs, less of its people would turn to communism for a solution of their problems?

I think very few people in the United States are turning

to communism as a solution to their problems. I am afraid that you will have to get over thinking that the United States is meddling in European affairs. The U.S. has a vital interest in affairs all over the world now, because without that interest the world cannot be stabilized, and we cannot prosper in an unsettled world.

There is no reason, however, why the United States should not give proper attention to helping people at home to a solution of their prejudices. There are no minority problems existing here except those due to prejudice, and the people themselves have to overcome those prejudices. The Government may help them by stimulating education on these subjects, by seeing that as a Government there is equal administration of justice and that equal opportunities are accorded to all people. These things will never become realities, however, except through the removal of prejudice from the hearts of all our people.

My daughter is a student in one of the local high schools. Before the Junior Prom this year a Negro student asked if she expected to attend. When she said "No," he told her he would like to take her if she would go with him. She thanked him, but told him she had made other plans for the evening. What would be your reaction to such a situation? Would you permit your daughter to attend a prom with a colored boy, or would you have felt, as I did, a little bit disconcerted at the idea of his even suggesting such a thing?

Your question is a difficult one to answer because there must be a background to it. If your daughter had known this young boy well, I do not think that it was in any way astonishing that he should ask her to go with him, because if they had been on a purely friendly acquaintanceship basis, there was no more reason why she should not go with him than with any one of the other boys whom she knew equally well.

What lies back of your feeling, of course, is the old fear of intermarriage between races. That is something I feel we have to deal with on an entirely different basis from mere friendly association. There may come a time when it will seem as natural to marry a man from any race, or any part of the world, as it will to marry your next-door neighbor. We haven't reached that time as yet, and there is still considerable feeling when people marry who have different religious backgrounds, and there is, of course, more feeling still about intermarriage between different races. So it seems to me that that question has to be dealt with individually, by families, by individuals and by society. At present intermarriage between races, and even between people of different religions, often brings reprisals from society and from families, which make for great unhappiness. Anyone undertaking such a marriage must have a full realization of what she is actually facing.

However, going to a prom is like any other casual thing which you do; and if we are not going to be able to have ordinary contacts with people who are citizens of our own country, how on earth can we expect that we will be able to have the same kind of contact with people who live in different parts of the world? I think we can have peace in our hearts and real friendship for people even though there may still be some fundamental reason why we would not marry. Therefore, if I were you I would not worry too much about the people with whom your daughter dances. I should hope that she could be unconsciously friendly with all her associates in school, and I would be rather proud that a boy of another race felt that he could ask your daughter to go to a prom—which shows, I think, that her attitude has been kind and mature.

I am twelve, and I live in the South, and this is my problem: My mother says I am too friendly with the colored girl who keeps my brothers and me. I think being nice toward her is the best way to return the helpful things she does for me and her niceness too. And how can I stop being friendly without maybe hurting her feelings?

My dear child, your mother is probably better able to tell you how to behave than I am. She certainly does not want you to hurt the feelings of anyone who is in her employ, but she may feel you are not quite wise in showing your desire to be helpful. Take your problem to your mother. She is far better able to help you than I am.

Do you think we should continue to admit former Nazi sympathizers like musician Walter Gieseking and singer Kirsten Flagstad to this country?

I can't say I think we should bar artists from this country today, no matter what their political backgrounds may have been. Flagstad is not going to sing about Nazism; neither is Mr. Gieseking going to do anything with his music that would taint it with Nazism. To bar artists because of beliefs they have held in the past, or even hold in the present, seems to me a loss to the artistic world—which is, of course, rarely a very political world.

My husband and I decided some years ago that our small contributions to peace would be never to tell or repeat "Eleanor stories," racial-prejudice stories or jokes, but we differ on our reactions to others' telling such stories. My husband says that if other persons make racial jokes, it is like beating your head against a stone wall to argue with them. He just changes the subject. I "light into" them, and tell them if they can't say anything good, not to say anything. Which of us is correct?

I doubt if "lighting into" people ever does much good, but I think the time has come when we ourselves must stand up and be counted for our beliefs. If we can say quietly that we think the attitude that someone is taking is harmful to the co-operation between people of different races and religions and will not help to promote peace in the world, and explain very calmly why we think so, we may plant a seed in even a prejudiced mind, which may of itself bear fruit someday.

14. on Public Questions

*Do you think the President of the United States should
be elected by direct vote of the people?*

Yes, on the whole, because I do not see why at the present
time we need to continue the old system of the electoral
college. Therefore, if I am given a chance to vote on the
subject I shall vote for the direct placing of the names
of the candidates for President on the ballot rather than
having to vote for electors.

*Why doesn't everyone in the United States have to pay
an income tax of at least five dollars? Don't you think
this would make everyone feel a sense of responsibility
as a citizen?*

I do not know why you set five dollars as the sum to be
paid. I think everyone should pay an income tax, but
there are some incomes so low that five dollars would be
almost impossible to accumulate during the year, so I

think everyone should pay a percentage of what he actually has earned during the year.

Isn't there any way a man in public office could be forced to have a psychiatric examination when his lies and vilifications of others are obviously psychopathic?

Who is to judge whether a man is psychopathic or not? If you do not happen to like things he says about others and you call them lies, others may think they are truthful. He may think so himself. It is very difficult to prove anyone psychopathic, and I hardly think we can take everybody who differs with us in our estimate of ourselves or of others and have them examined by a psychiatrist.

Don't you think some control should be established by the Government over freedom of the press when this freedom is abused and used for political propaganda to the extent it is in this country? What part can the individual citizen play in achieving this control?

I am afraid if we started trying to control the press, we might really do away with an essential freedom. It is true that this freedom is often abused, but I think the basis of democracy is that we educate people sufficiently well so that they can be trusted, in the long run, to judge political propaganda and the type of news that is slanted by certain types of interests. The individual citizen can best control the press by insisting always that the papers in his own home environment write uncolored news stories.

A columnist who has been branded as a warmonger insists a third world war is inevitable. How does this fit in

*with freedom of speech and the press? Should we give
certain sensationalists the opportunity to talk us into another war?*

I doubt if any columnist can talk us into war. If we
curtail their right to speak, we could not speak ourselves
against some of their statements. Freedom of speech
and of the press is essential to all of us, but education
and a thinking public are also essential, because where
there is a freedom of expression, there must always be
an ability on the part of the listeners to think and to
sift the good from the bad of that which one hears or
reads.

*Recently my husband, who manages and partly owns a
small business, has been threatened in an effort to stop
him from shipping to a market which one of our national labor organizations is attempting to organize.
Would you state your feelings about such tactics?*

So many different situations present themselves in labor
disputes that it is well to have the precise situation de-
scribed before venturing an answer. There undoubtedly
are situations in which unions are unreasonable. On
the other hand, there are situations which too often are
denounced as unreasonable when they are not unreasonable at all. Many businessmen realize that when
unions refuse to handle products which are manufac-
tured under low wages, long hours and poor working
conditions, the decent employer is being helped. A good
employer should not be subjected to competition by
other employers who underprice him by reason of their
exploitation of workers. The situation confronting
your husband may be one in which his support of the

union position would eventually result in his own profit.

Do you think that labor unions should have the right to participate in determining what industrial prices and profits should be?

I think we are coming probably to a period where our old ideas are going to change somewhat. There was a time when we thought it was nobody's business but the individuals' how much they worked, or under what conditions they worked, or how much profit an employer made, or what was charged to the consumer for the goods that were on the market. As we have developed, we think it is within our rights to know under what conditions any work is performed, and whether the wages paid make it possible for a family to maintain a decent standard of living. If we are interested in that, it goes without saying that we are interested in finding out whether a business can really pay these wages. We can only do that as we know what the recompense of management is, what the profits are to management and to the stockholders, what the remuneration is for distribution and whether the ultimate price to the consumer is a fair one or too much of a mark-up.

It should not be just labor unions and management who are interested in these questions. It should be the public as a whole, and the information should be available to any citizen. In fact, it seems to me quite fair that reports should be given on negotiations of contracts between labor and management, since all these points should come up for consideration, and those who are going to buy should be as interested as the people who are to perform the work and the people who own the business and are going to profit by what is sold.

In my state only 8 per cent of the feeble-minded are in institutions. Do you believe the remaining 92 per cent who are at large should be allowed to produce children three times as fast as normal citizens? Would it not be better to sterilize the mentally deficient and prevent children from being born to feeble-minded parents?

I have always felt that in some way the objectives you are suggesting should be achieved. Just how to do it is the difficulty, since some states do not have the proper legislation, and in other cases there are religious scruples to be encountered, but it seems quite terrible to allow the mentally unfit to continue to have children.

Do you believe that any government or religious agency should have the right to censor movies?

I happen not to like the idea of censorship, except such censorship as the people exercise when they ignore something, and personally I feel in the long run we would be better off if we relied on the industries themselves and the public to do the necessary censoring.

I have heard that the social security laws make it more expensive for employers to hire old people than young ones. Is this true?

This same fear has been expressed as regards workmen's compensation, which is the earliest form of what we now call social security in this country. Most experts now believe that while it may take longer for older people to recover from injuries which they sustain at work, they do not sustain as many injuries as younger people because they are more careful. Therefore, these experts believe the net result is that it is less expensive for employers to hire old people than young ones.

As regards unemployment insurance, which was the next form of social security to go into effect in this country, it may be argued that older persons who are laid off have more difficulty finding another job than young people, so that an employer's contribution rate might be slightly higher. However, offsetting this possibility is that the turnover among older workers is usually less, so that the cost of breaking in new workers is reduced. Moreover, many times older workers possess greater skill and are more careful than younger workers, so that the quality of their output is higher.

In the case of old-age insurance, which is the latest form of social security, there is no question that this enables employers to hire older workers without the danger of incurring greater expenses in providing retirement benefits. This is so well recognized that employers as well as labor organizations generally support the extension and improvement of our federal old-age survivors insurance law.

Why are farmers singled out for subsidies while other businessmen—lawyers, for example—are left to shift for themselves?

Because the farmers are engaged in a basic occupation. If the farmers were not willing to continue their work the rest of us would starve. The farmers are engaged in probably the most exciting gamble that there is as a business venture. They gamble with the unpredictable whims of nature. The government, knowing that people must eat, tries to reduce the dangers which may overtake those who engage in this hazardous occupation of farming.

Do you not think that persons deserve a trial by jury before being committed to a state mental hospital?

I hardly think a trial by jury for mentally disturbed patients would have much value, because the jury would probably not be made up of people with much medical knowledge. I do think, however, that before people are permanently committed to a mental hospital there should be a consultation with doctors, some of them not connected with the family or the hospital, to insure that the individual gets proper consideration of his particular case.

Is it true you were opposed to capital punishment for the people who murdered Bobby Greenlease? If you don't think kidnap-murderers should get the death sentence, what do you think they should get?

I have never said I was opposed to capital punishment in any single case. I have said I was opposed to capital punishment in general, because it does not achieve the results we hope for. Many who have been in prison work their entire lives are convinced that capital punishment does not discourage crime, and many countries which have done away with it have found their crime conditions did not become worse but in some cases better. I think it is evident, therefore, that it is not the best kind of punishment for the worst crimes.

Socialized medicine has been tried in England and France and in other countries under different systems of administration. What are your views on Government control in this field in the United States?

I believe the Government should improve its Public Health Service. I believe it could also aid in a better distribution of doctors in areas where at present there are none. I believe that the Government could aid in building hospitals and clinics where they are needed, by grants to communities. I do not know that we have found the best way of getting the best possible medical care for all our people. I think we should try whatever is suggested until we find that we have something which works well, because it is essential that medical care be accessible for all at a moderate cost where people can pay, and free where they cannot. A healthy nation is essential for future strength.

Why are you always so much on the side of the arrogant, sometimes communistic labor leaders rather than on the side of the millions of men thrown out of work for long periods by the acts of those leaders and their inter-union quarrels?

I did not know that I was on the side of arrogant, communistic labor leaders. There are some labor leaders in whom I believe, and I do not consider them either arrogant or communistic. There are other labor leaders whom I dislike thoroughly, but for a variety of reasons. I am always on the side of men who are out of work, and particularly of their families, who have to stand a good deal of suffering under those conditions.

Do you approve of the peacetime draft?

At the present time I do because conditions in the world are so unsettled. I think the knowledge that we are willing to submit to military training for a great number of our young people will undoubtedly have a stabilizing effect in parts of the world where a threat might exist to the peace of the world. I hope very much, however, that we will bend every effort to build up international strength in the United Nations, and that as soon as possible not only the peacetime draft will be dropped, but general disarmament will begin. Joint strength acquired by the United Nations, when it is strong enough to insure the peace of the world, whether a great or a small nation chooses to create trouble, is the only way to bring about national disarmament and leave us free to devote our resources to social developments for the greater happiness of all people.

15. on History

Will you please tell me and the other children in the
sixth grade who you think were the five greatest people
in the world? I mean who contributed most to the world.

Christ, Confucius, Mohammed, Buddha and Plato. Any
list of this kind is of necessity very poor, because I have
not defined "greatness." Greatness lies in many different fields, and the contribution of people to the world
is made in a great variety of fields, but these are the
men who spiritually have led us in the past and probably
shaped much of the thinking of the world.

Which do you consider the five greatest American presidents?

Washington, Jefferson, Jackson, Lincoln and my own
husband, Franklin D. Roosevelt. Though it is early to
assess in a historical way a man's greatness, still I feel
that the problems my husband met and solved will make
the period of history he lived in a great period, and there-

fore I believe history will feel that he was one of our great Presidents.

Will you perhaps suggest a half dozen or so books that you might call required reading on the American scene for those like myself who have come to this country as the wives of American servicemen? I came here from a small village in England and there is so much I have to learn of this country I now call "home."

If you can get Dorothy Canfield's Hillsboro People and Edith Wharton's Ethan Frome, you will get a fair picture of New England. Carl Carmer's books will give you the background of New York State. To get the foundations of the wild and woolly west, you might read Bret Harte's The Luck of Roaring Camp. There are many charming stories of the South, but Gone With the Wind will give you a picture of the Civil War and its aftermath. If you will read Whittier's poems, and Walt Whitman's, and in addition some of the biographies of people like Washington, Jefferson, Lincoln by Carl Sandburg, you will get the flavor of the men whose ideals have built this country.

In the light of your son's recent book, were the relations between your husband and Prime Minister Churchill misrepresented as true friendship to the American people? If not, why has your son written at this time such tactless statements about the successful accomplishments of two great leaders?

I do not think you read my son's book very carefully. He explains that there existed between my husband and Prime Minister Churchill a warm personal friendship, and I have done this also in a column which I wrote on this particular subject. There can be a warm personal friendship between two individuals who, because of background and the circumstances under which they have lived, may have entirely different political beliefs, and very different approaches to the ultimate objectives which they wish to achieve through government. That, I think, was really the case where my husband and Mr. Churchill were concerned. As far as the war period went, each knew that the other was a good man, leading his people well and acting wisely to meet the needs of the war situation.

I think my husband understood and admired Mr. Churchill's patriotism and his devotion to his country. My husband had an equally patriotic devotion to the United States of America. He considered that the interests of the two countries were not always identical. There were political interests entering the war strategy here and there that were bound to cause some differences. Even more difficulties are certain to appear in times of peace.

I do not feel that my son made any tactless statements. He knew quite well where the areas of cooperation and warm affection existed and also where the difficulties lay and what caused them.

All these years I have tried to find out why Japan got our scrap iron while fighting China and right up to Pearl Harbor. There was a law by which the President could have legally stopped this, and even without it the American people would have backed up our President Roosevelt.

If you will read Secretary Hull's book you will, I think, recognize the difficulties we faced in our diplomatic position with Japan prior to Pearl Harbor. There were a great many people in this country who felt that by our belligerent attitude we were forcing Japan into going to war with us. Our government officials feared that if we refused to continue trading with Japan she might use that as a pretext for going to war with us. Quite naturally we were anxious, if it were possible, to prevent war with Japan while a war was going on in Europe. One of the things our students of military strategy feared more than anything else was war in two parts of the world, and that is the situation into which Japan's attack finally forced us. That is the only reason why our officials, after much thought, decided to continue trading with Japan and the supply of scrap iron was accumulated even though we knew it would come back at us in very unpleasant ways if war actually came. Though my memory is no longer accurate on this I have heard it said that every month we gave scrap iron to Japan, and thereby delayed Japan's entry into the war, we increased our productive capacity to such an extent that it probably put us four months ahead in our preparation for war.

Don't you feel that the American people were misled in accepting the Four Freedoms as ideals to fight for, and don't you think our boys who died for them died in vain?

No. I do not think the American people were misled any more than they were misled by our forefathers who wrote the Constitution and the Bill of Rights. We haven't yet achieved everything that was set down in the Constitution as our ultimate objective, but it did not hurt us any to have it set down, and it gives us something to strive for, and many people have died for these aims. Every time that we get a step nearer to the great conception that our forefathers had, we justify the faith of those who died, and this is true of a belief in the Four Freedoms and in the hope of their ultimate realization.

Early in August, 1940, when Mr. Hopkins visited Stalin at Moscow he committed this country to furnish Russia with certain armaments of great magnitude. Why was not the matter of payments for such critical goods taken up, agreed upon, the signatures affixed and sealed: Russia to pay in gold to the limit of her ability, then in raw materials, which she had in abundance before Lend-Lease was put in operation? In other words, why did we not deal with Russia on the same basis as we did with Great Britain in this respect?

Harry Hopkins did not go to Russia in 1940. At that time the Soviet Union was in effect allied with Hitler's Germany and Mussolini's Italy. The American Communist party was then picketing the White House. Russia was denouncing President Roosevelt for every measure that he took to give aid to Great Britain, which was then alone in fighting the Axis powers.

In June, 1941, Hitler attacked the Soviet Union, and a month later Hopkins flew from Britain to Moscow for his first meeting with Stalin. At these meetings (which are fully recorded in the book *Roosevelt and Hopkins*) Hopkins attempted to learn Stalin's estimate of Russia's chances for survival and of her principal material needs. He had no authority to make any commitments as to supplies for Russia from the United States, and he made none. He reported back to President Roosevelt and Prime Minister Churchill when they met at the Atlantic Conference in August, 1941.

At the end of September of that year an Anglo-American mission was sent to Moscow to draw up an agreement for supplies to be sent from the United States and Great Britain to aid the Russian war effort. Hopkins was not a member of this mission, which was headed by Lord Beaverbrook and Averell Harriman. From that time on the supplies that went to Russia from the United States were in accordance with the terms of the Lend-Lease law and, therefore, on the same basis as the supplies that went to Great Britain and other Allied countries.

Do you not think that loving and trusting President Roosevelt, we, the constituents back home, influenced Congress to grant extraordinary powers to the President under his administration, and which are beyond the intended limitations of that office wisely outlined in the Constitution of the United States?

No, I do not think it was affection for President Roosevelt which made you influence Congress to grant extraordinary powers to the President. Those were granted him because the domestic conditions when he came into office were so chaotic he had to have such powers in order to carry out programs which would change the trend which was bringing complete despair to most of the citizens of the United States. Later, when the war was upon us, conditions again were such that the President had to have extraordinary powers. You would have had to grant these powers in both cases to anyone who was forced to pull the United States out of the difficulties in which she was engulfed during the depression and to steer her through the worst war in her history. The Constitution was written so as to permit of interpretations to meet whatever might come in the future. One cannot write such a rigid Constitution that when new circumstances arise it cannot be applied. The value of our Constitution lies in its extreme flexibility, and Congress is free, when it feels certain powers are not needed, to withdraw them.

16. on Politics

Somebody has defined a liberal by calling him "a radical with a wife and two children." That definition doesn't satisfy me, and I can't think of any other which does—especially in these times. How would you state the liberal position?

It is very difficult to put into words the liberal position, but I would be inclined to say that a liberal tries to see a question from as many points of view as possible and then decide which is the point of view which will benefit the greatest number of people. He need not be either conservative or radical, but he must be able to be objective, to try to free himself from prejudice and to subordinate his own special interests to the interests of the people as a whole.

As a Republican who respects your opinion I am writing to ask you if you don't really think Eisenhower has done a good job as President so far?

It is very difficult to say, because one does not know yet exactly where the President will eventually stand. Some of the trends of this administration—for instance, the trend to return to private ownership everything in the way of national resources, so that the government has no check on the conservation or distribution of these resources—seem to me to be dangerous trends. The President's attitude on Senator McCarthy also seems to me not yet sufficiently clear. But, as I said, it is too early to form any clear estimate.

I would like to know how you feel Secretary of State Dulles' performance to date compares with that of former Secretary of State Acheson.

I happen to think that history will consider Secretary Acheson a great Secretary of State. It is much too early as yet to evaluate what Secretary Dulles will be able to do during his term of office.

Please explain why it is that the nineteenth-century liberals fought for the liberation of the individual from the control of the state or government, while today's liberals seem to be always on the side of more government controls over the individual.

Because in the nineteenth century the individual had comparatively few liberties. There was no recognition that the government owed an individual certain things as a right. There were charities, but at that time the government was not conceived as doing away with charity. Now it is accepted that the government has an obligation to guard the rights of an individual so carefully that he never reaches a point which needs charity.

Nowadays the government controls which are advocated by the liberals are all to safeguard, in a modern and very complicated world, some of the things which individuals have come to feel they have a right to achieve. For instance, we insist that the government must see that every man who wants to work is able to get work suitable to his ability and at a wage on which he and his family can live. The nineteenth-century liberals did not have to face that problem and therefore no regulation was needed. Regulations have come only as our complicated civilization has made them necessary.

What is your definition of "McCarthyism"?

It is the habit of accusing people without proof and of doing it through clever falsification. If you will look up the documented presentation by Senator Benton in support of his resolution to oust McCarthy from the Senate you will see how, by taking portions of something that has been said from one place and tacking it on to something from somewhere else, a completely false impression is created. In other words, "the unproved smear based on falsification" is my definition of McCarthyism.

How much truth do you think there is in your son John's statement that if your husband were living today he'd be ashamed of the Democratic party?

In all the years of my husband's political life I never remember hearing him make such a rash statement; therefore, I would hesitate to say what he might feel if he were with us today.

What are the disadvantages, if any, of a democratic government such as ours?

One of the disadvantages is that reforms which are necessary come slowly. However, perhaps this is not entirely a disadvantage, because it arises from the fact that not just a few individuals but the great mass of the people must be educated to understand and desire reform. When that happens and the reform comes about, the support for it is on a very firm foundation which, though it may seem to some of us one of the drawbacks of democracy, is perhaps in the end a strength. It is undeniably true that a benevolent despot can quickly bring about better conditions and avoid suffering for the people as a whole, but one cannot always count on a despot being benevolent! However, the one thing I think we can count on is the slow but sure education of the people in their own interests.

Have you ever voted Republican?

No, I have never voted Republican because women did not have a vote prior to 1920. In 1912 I attended meetings and would have voted for Theodore Roosevelt had women been allowed to vote at that time. Since that time I have never voted for a Republican candidate because I never felt that on the whole the Republican candidate was better than the Democratic candidate.

Did you know anything about your husband's reported plan to establish a new party of liberal Republicans and Democrats with Wendell Willkie?

I know nothing about such a plan. My husband may have talked with Mr. Willkie, as he did with many other people, about the possibility of new party line-ups. The two parties, Republican and Democratic, today are similarly divided, with reactionaries in both parties. We used to discuss the possibility of getting a clear-cut liberal party to oppose a clear-cut reactionary party.

In his recent book Judge Rosenman says that if you had been given your way there would have been fewer compromises and fewer accomplishments on the part of the New Deal. Can you explain this remark?

Of course, I think Judge Rosenman could probably explain better than I can. I can only imagine that he meant what my husband often said to me—that I was much too impatient to be a good politician, that I wanted to see results much too quickly and therefore would sometimes perhaps have accepted the attitude of a benevolent despot rather than have had the patience to wait for democratic forces to work out the problems and solutions far more slowly. With age I have become more patient!

In your opinion what is the basic difference between a Democrat and a Republican today?

It is very difficult to state in a few words the basic difference between the two parties today. My own feeling is that both parties are split, and the old idea that one is liberal and the other conservative can no longer be held, because there is a conservative element in both parties. The basic thing, I think, to those of us who prefer the Democratic to the Republican party is the fact the record shows that progress in legislation has largely been proposed and passed during Democratic administrations. So we feel there is a greater number of progressive people in the Democratic party.

*How do you feel about some of the Republican Senators'
proposals to drop the atom bomb if our negotiations do
not achieve peace in the Far East?*

> I have very little hope that dropping the atom bomb
> would achieve peace, and I am afraid it would bring us
> the dislike of other nations and create a fear which would
> not be beneficial to peaceful relations.

*Do you feel that the candidate or the party is the more
important issue in an election?*

> That is a very difficult question to answer. As a rule I feel
> that even a very fine man can do very little against the
> party that has a well-organized machinery and clear-cut
> objectives. Therefore, ordinarily I consider the party
> more important than the man. But this would not hold
> if the man were clearly incompetent or had some moral
> or mental quality that one disapproved of fundamentally.

17. on Communism

*Some people think a course in Communism should be
taught in our schools. How do you feel about this?*

I think it would be extremely helpful to young people
to understand the basis of Communism, the Party line
and the Party tactics.

*What in your opinion is the greater danger in Commu-
nism—atheism or its economic aims?*

It is very difficult to answer questions of this kind, because what I really object to most in Communism is not
some of the theories—which were written by Karl Marx
in an attempt to correct some of the injustices that he
saw during the Industrial Revolution in England—but
rather the way Communism developed under Stalin.

Trying to make Stalin and the Communist party take
the place of God has not succeeded even with many
Russian people, and it seems to me that it would be
almost impossible to wipe out religion by offering Com-

munism in its place unless people had already lost their faith in their religion.

What I really consider the greatest danger in Communism is its creation of a police state, which puts everybody under such terror that there is no free expression of individual thinking and no dignity for the human being. The evil of Communism as it has developed in Europe is, of course, the same evil which existed in Fascism and Nazism.

Did the late President Roosevelt ever express to you any suspicion or alarm about Communists in the State Department?

I don't remember my husband ever expressing suspicion about people in the State Department. If he were suspicious of anyone he would not have spoken to me but to Secretary Hull.

As for alarms, if my husband thought a situation was dangerous he immediately took the steps he considered necessary. He did not indulge in expressing alarms or fears.

One of my grandson's professors tells his classes that the Committee on Un-American Activities is ruining our reputation in the rest of the world. First, Mrs. Roosevelt, do you think there's any truth in this? Secondly, should a man be permitted to say such things in the classroom?

Yes, I think this professor's statement is absolutely correct. As for his right to make the statement, if it is proper for an individual to hold opinions it seems to me proper for him to state them in the classroom, as long as they are not directed against the welfare of the country and do not advocate the overthrow of the government by force.

Why doesn't the President order the FBI to give all the information on suspected Communists in the government to the Senate Investigating Committee?

Probably because it would be unwise to do so. FBI investigations are made by agents who collect all kinds of information from all kinds of people—both reliable and unreliable. To be properly understood this must be screened and evaluated by trained people. If you turn a complete file over to a Senate Investigating Committee you are asking untrained people to take over a job which requires experts to do it properly. By exposing all this material to the public you are also, of course, revealing methods of the FBI to certain people who should not know anything about these methods.

You said recently that a Congressional investigation of schools and colleges won't accomplish anything except scare everybody to death. Does this mean you don't think any Communists are teaching in our schools? Please explain yourself.

I have no idea how many Communists may or may not be teaching in our schools and colleges, but I think the Congressional investigation is likely to be much less effective than a careful survey by the heads of school systems and colleges and universities themselves. They are certainly better fitted to do this kind of house-cleaning than the members of the Un-American Activities Committee, and they are less likely to create mistrust and suspicion. When a teacher is called to testify before a

Congressional committee nowadays it has a demoraliz-
ing effect on other faculty members and on students.

*How would you feel about an investigation of Commu-
nists among the clergy?*
I would feel it outrageous.

*If you were asked to testify publicly about a friend who
had once been a member of the Communist party but
was now a loyal American, and you knew such testimony
would cost him his job, what would you do?*
Ordinarily if I knew a man had once been a Communist
I would not hesitate to say so—and to add that I knew
he was now a loyal citizen. But if I were dealing with
such a hysterical situation that a statement of this kind
would cost this man his chance to earn a living, and if
I knew of no overriding reason for giving such testimony,
I would refuse to give it.

*I am a frightened and bewildered mother. Frightened
because the radio and newspapers give us nothing to look
forward to but atomic warfare. I cannot understand why
this nation, founded by men fleeing from a government
they thought wrong, can tell other countries what kind
of government to set up. Isn't keeping communism from
spreading in this country a big enough fight?*
I think it would be well for all of us to stop talking about
keeping communism from spreading and talk about
making democracy a success. If it is going to succeed,
your part in its success will be in making your own surroundings thoroughly successful in the use of the democratic processes, both in everyday living and in the po-

litical and economic life of your environment. If enough people do this, the success of democracy will be self-evident.

We must bend every effort to create a successful democracy here, because we believe people have greater control themselves politically under a democratic system, and we are convinced that from the economic standpoint a capitalistic system with proper democratic controls can give people more opportunity and greater satisfaction than can a communist system.

I have heard that the graduates of certain colleges have trouble finding jobs because people believe there is a communistic trend in those institutions. What is your opinion about this?

I think people should not accept offhand rumors about educational institutions. They should investigate. I think they would frequently find that there is no basis for the rumors, in which case they should not be affected by them. They should judge the person to be engaged on his performance and not on any rumor of any kind.

Why should a citizen of this country who is a member of the Communist Party claim, because of free speech, more power to work against his country than if he were a communist living in Russia?

I do not think that a communist living in this country has any more opportunity to work against our Government than the rest of us have to work for it. We can talk just as well as a communist can talk, and if we let him get away with talking more, we are to blame. A communist living in Russia is, of course, more effective because he talks about something which everyone around him knows exists and believes in. A communist talking in this country is talking to a receptive audience only when we have failed to make democracy work. I believe in free speech, and I am not really afraid that our people cannot be trusted to see the disadvantages of communism as long as we perfect the democratic processes at home.

Would it not be possible to outlaw the Communist Party in the United States, although we are supposed to be a free country where everyone can express his convictions?

I think it would be highly unwise to outlaw the Communist Party in the United States. How would you feel if you were a citizen of the U.S.S.R. and decided that you preferred to have a more democratic form of government and you were outlawed because of it? That is practically what would happen to you in Russia today, but that has never happened to us in the United States. We are a free country, we can express our convictions with only the limitation of not advocating the overthrow of the Government by force. We can use all the persuasion that lies in our power. We trust, however, that democracy will so completely meet the needs of the people that there will always be among us people who believe strongly enough in it to fight for it with words and by deeds. We must prove that the people's well-being is satisfactory because of the way we use our democracy and that there is no value in making any change.

I have found out that a man and woman who are my
friends are active communists. They have a store. Know-
ing their sympathies, I have stopped patronizing them.
However, the rest of the neighborhood continue to shop
there, knowing they are communists. Am I doing wrong
mixing business with politics?

Communists have a right to earn a living in the United
States as long as we permit them to be here. We have
an obligation to allow people to think and peacefully
communicate their thoughts to others as long as they do
not attempt to overthrow the Government by force. For
that reason the fact that people who run stores and gain
a livelihood believe in certain theories which we do not
believe in is no reason, from my point of view, for not
associating with them. It may, however, become disagreeable to have contacts with them because you feel
you are helping them to promote something in which
you do not believe. In that case, you will naturally not
continue your contacts. That will be for personal reasons and not because of their political views only.

Up until now my husband and I have considered our-
selves good Americans. Now I feel our rights as Ameri-
cans are threatened because my mother and stepfather
belong to the Communist party. What is to become of
us and our twelve-year-old son? Will he be branded too
because his grandmother is a Communist? What can
we do to prove that we are good Americans?

Your situation is a difficult one, but there is, of course,
no reason why you should suffer because of the ideas
held by your mother and stepfather and certainly no

reason why your twelve-year-old son should suffer. During the present state of mind in this country I suppose it is hard for people to think of members of a family as individuals, but it must be done. The only thing you can do is to continue to live as a good American and to insist that you do not hold communist theories and therefore should not be condemned merely by association with your mother.

If most of the members of the American Youth Congress had refused to answer by invoking the Fifth Amendment when you questioned them about their Communist affiliations, would you have continued working with them?

They could not have invoked the Fifth Amendment in talking with me, because I had no authority to demand an answer from them. I was asking them simply to be honest with me, as a friend of young people. When their actions proved that certain leaders were under Communist domination and could hoodwink many of the followers I did refuse to work with them.

In your opinion what group or groups in the U.S. are putting up the best fight against Communism?

Labor, the liberals and all those who understand that Communism is fed by misery and despair and are working to prevent that kind of misery and despair from spreading in the world.

18. on Soviet Russia

---

*I'm told that if Karl Marx's theories had been practiced
as he intended, Russia would not be a dictatorship today.
Can you explain this statement to me?*

Karl Marx, like all important thinkers, has produced
many schools of followers. All of them claim him as
their inspiration while they violently disagree with one
another. The moderate socialists in pre-revolutionary
Russia—the Menshiviks, whom the Bolsheviks sup-
pressed—were vigorously opposed to the concept of dictatorship, and they also claimed they were Marxists.
Many of the moderate socialist parties in Europe today
who are violently anticommunist venerate Karl Marx.

We must remember that Marx wrote in England in
opposition to the hardships he saw brought about by the
then existing economic system. That was a time of great
industrial distress. We might compare it to the depression days we ourselves have known and look upon Marx's
feelings in comparison with the way we used to feel

when we saw lines of men waiting for a handout of a cup of coffee and a bun perhaps in some of our big cities. We must also remember that Karl Marx is used by the communists who follow his doctrines and tailor them to fit the particular interpretation which they desire.

Now that you have seen what happened to Mr. Robert Vogeler, have you revised your opinion of Cardinal Mindszenty?

I never had any opinion of Cardinal Mindszenty, so I could not very well revise it. I have stated a number of times that I dislike the type of trial conducted in the communist-controlled countries and above everything else I dislike trials which have anything to do with the question of a person's religion. I did add, however, that the case of Cardinal Mindszenty in Hungary was slightly complicated by the fact that the Roman Catholic Church had been one of the largest land owners, if not the largest, in Hungary. This does not affect the Cardinal as a person, but anyone who knows European history knows that this has led to trouble in European countries before. Such a situation is not a religious but a secular one.

I do not think anyone has any faith in the justice of trials in communist-controlled countries, whether they are trials of members of any religion (lately some of the Mormons and Baptists have been in trouble) or whether they are trials of business people accused of political activity, as in the case of Mr. Vogeler. Justice as we know it in the United States is simply not practiced in these communist-controlled countries, and we cannot expect it.

You have worked closely with Soviet delegates to the
U.N. Do you think the Russians now—or ever—have
made a genuine peace offer?

> That is extremely difficult to tell. It may be that from
> their point of view the offers are genuine. They do not
> seem genuine to us because the Russians have never
> been willing to accept safeguards which we consider
> essential, or to permit an international commission to
> see whether their promises will be carried out.

Since you are considered an intelligent and farsighted
woman, do you think that the Roman Catholic Church
plans to maneuver us into a war with Russia by trying
to get people of that faith into key positions within our
government and throughout the world?

> No, I do not think the Roman Catholic Church is try-
> ing to maneuver us into another war. It is true that
> probably the two great disciplines of the world are the
> Communist discipline and the Jesuit discipline, which is
> a fact pointed out by a Frenchman brought up by the
> Jesuits. I think the Roman Catholic Church should do
> all it can to reduce the strength of communism, but I
> do not think it would want to see any nation go to war.

The Soviet Union brags so much about the status of its
women. What is your impression of the Soviet delegates
you've seen?

> I do not happen to have seen a woman who had the
> status of delegate since the first meeting of the General
> Assembly in London. This particular woman was very
> intelligent and a pleasure to work with. There are
> women, however, in other positions on the Soviet dele-

gation, and if the treatment meted out to them, as one casually observes it, is a sign of equality, it is not, from my point of view, what the women in the United States would like. I have seen a delegate hand his heavy brief-case to his wife to carry. I am sure that the Soviet delegates would give either a man or a woman only the consideration he or she could exact. From what the Russians say, however, I am sure that women receive equal treatment—on paper at any rate—with the men.

Of all the lies the Communists have told the people of Europe about Americans, which do you feel are most widely accepted as the truth?

That we are imperialist and trying to conquer the world through control of the economies of countries; that we are not interested in humanitarian services but only make believe that we are; that they are anxious for peace and we want war.

Why is there so much hysteria against Russia, but seldom any criticism of Fascist Spain or Argentina? Isn't it because whenever a country adopts socialism or communism it is closed to further exploitation by American monopolies?

No, I do not think there is hysteria against Russia. There are perfectly valid criticisms of the U.S.S.R. for certain practices with which we do not agree. There are also valid criticisms of fascism as it appeared in Spain and as it has appeared in the Argentine.

I do not think that today American manufacturers are exploiting any part of the world in the way many interests did two or three decades ago. Exploitation is more difficult for any nation, but it is certainly not because the nation has adopted communism or socialism that this is the case. I would be inclined to say that in the case of communism it is the communist government which does the exploiting, and there is no citizen to do much criticizing. If any of our monopolies, so-called, were to try to do much exploiting in a socialist or democratic state there would be plenty of criticism.

The Russian delegates to the U.N. seem very cold and inhuman in their public appearances, but I understand that in private many of them are very pleasant and amusing. Have you found this to be true? Which ones especially?

I have had very few occasions on which to discover whether any of the Russian delegates are different in private from what they are in public. A few of them have dined with me, usually with an interpreter sitting behind their chairs. A few have spent evenings in my sitting room and on such occasions have been pleasant guests. They have always been courteous when they came, but they are nearly always impersonal and always very guarded in their remarks, never forgetting that they are government representatives and cannot speak in a personal capacity.

I had the great fortune to escape from a mad and bloody Germany and it took long to overcome bitterness and an inferiority complex. But I feel double the responsibility to work for peace. Stronger and stronger grows the conviction within me that it must be the mission of the women to unite against war. Do you think it possible to reach the Russian women?

I doubt that we can find a way to reach the Russian

women at the present time. Communications are very difficult between our two countries, information is restricted and friendship is not encouraged.

I wish it were not so, but I feel that any effort to break the barriers down would be looked upon with a good deal of suspicion and be entirely unsuccessful.

The Russians invited English and American industrialists to Moscow and fed them all kinds of Soviet propaganda. Why don't we return the invitation and ask Russian labor leaders to visit this country? If they accept, they'll find out what lies they have been told at home. If they refuse, this fact would be worth publicizing in Europe.

I think it would be an excellent thing to do, but I do not know whether they would be convinced by anything they saw. They are so accustomed to having things made to look different from what they are for a purpose. I think it would not be strange if they thought we created a special kind of environment for them if they came over here.

What, if anything, do you believe the Americans and Russians have in common?

Many things. They are all human beings, and all human beings love and hate, are hungry or satisfied, tired or rested, ill or well, and all human beings have the same desire to live in peace, to have just and fair government which allows them to develop to the best of their ability. The differences come in the circumstances which surround human beings, and that is immediately where you come to the differences between the Americans and Russians.

19. on War and Peace

Do you think the invention of the atomic bomb has advanced or retarded civilization?

I think it advanced civilization in that it saved for us a great many young lives of a great many different nationalities which might otherwise have been lost in this period and therefore would have retarded the development of civilization. Whether in the future it is an aid to civilization depends on the scientists and our younger generation. Both groups know its potentialities for destruction.

Don't you think that wars, for the purpose of grabbing territory, are caused mainly by overpopulation? Could women's organizations in various countries get together on a program of "No population race for military purposes," in your opinion?

No. I do not think women could get together and have any such foolish program succeed. Neither do I think that wars are caused mainly because of overpopulation. Take a look at Russia, for instance—she certainly is not crowded; and there is plenty of untenanted land right in our own country, and yet we are tempted to take land for protective purposes or for trade development.

In recent months I have heard people talking about the "next war" as if it were inevitable. What is your opinion of people who talk like that?

I think they are very foolish people who really have no conception of what the next war would bring. We have been exceptionally fortunate in not having war on our own doorsteps. Our men have gone out to fight in faraway places and we have known anxiety and loss, but we have not known what bombs dropped on our own soil would mean, and perhaps that is why certain people feel free to talk about the next war. Even without the atomic bomb, destruction with our modern means of warfare is far too great to contemplate another war with equanimity. War can no longer be considered civilized.

How does the H-bomb alter the chances for world peace?

I think the H-bomb helps to remove the chances of war, because our scientists recognize that the H-bomb may be a completely destructive weapon. That means, of course, that the U.S.S.R. scientists also know this, and I have an idea that the Politburo is quite as anxious to continue to have a world in which to live as we are.

If experimentation with the H-bomb means possible destruction, it may prove the greatest incentive to keeping us at peace. I think this might be emphasized more than it is at the present time.

I am in the eighth grade, and my class is having a debate
on the question why don't we just drop the atomic bomb
on Russia before they drop it on us? I would appreciate it
if you would answer my letter.

There is a very simple answer to your question. The
country that uses an atom bomb in an undeclared war
will be the most hated country in the world, and no
one in that country will ever sleep without fear of re-
prisal. A great deal of destruction can be brought about,
and a great many innocent people can be killed by
dropping a bomb on Russia, but a country such as the
Soviet Union, where the people are scattered over the
land, would not suffer as we would here in the United
States, with our population so highly concentrated in
large cities.

What do you think is the greatest single cause of mis-
understanding between the nations of the world, both
great and small?

Fear.

Whom do you fear most in the world today?

I do not think I fear anyone.

20. on Foreign Policy

What, in your opinion, will happen to the financial structure of this country if we continue aiding the European countries, who, for the most part, have already taken all but a few remaining steps to communism? Nobody in Washington seems to consider the eventual end to our continually mounting Federal deficit.

There are a great many countries in Europe who have not taken any steps toward communism. Socialism is not communism—in fact, it is very far from it.

The real value of aid to existing democracies is that they must get on their feet, since chaos and despair are the way to force acceptance of economic communism. If democracies do not make a comeback in the economic field, we will find ourselves facing a constantly increasing area of communism in the world.

I wonder if you have given much thought to what that would mean to our economy. Our only hope of preserving for our people their present standard of living lies in bringing the countries of Western Europe back to economic stability in order that they may be politically stable as well. In Eastern Europe, communism is the answer they have chosen—and perhaps it is the only possible answer to their economic plight—but with our aid it should not be forced on those who have known other standards.

People in Washington are considering very carefully the mounting Federal deficit, but have you considered what would happen if you faced a completely communist Europe? This mounting Federal deficit, as it looks today, would look like a golden age to us.

How do you feel about having an American ambassador at the Vatican?

My personal feeling is that there may be value in having close contacts with the Pope. He is a great spiritual leader, and he has contacts in many parts of the world. But I do not see why we need an ambassador or minister. The personal representative with the rank of ambassador worked very well in one of the most difficult times in our history, and it seems to me that on that basis we maintained a cordial and close relationship with the Pope himself.

Moreover it is my understanding that in any exchange of ambassadors with the Vatican a concordat must be signed and the representative of the Pope automatically becomes senior member of the Diplomatic Corps. (This is the reason, I believe, that the United Kingdom has a minister and not an ambassador.) In a Catholic country the status of the Pope's ambassador presents no difficulties. In our country I think it would be difficult to observe this particular priority.

What did you find that the Indian and Arabic people
like most about the United States? What do they like
least?

One cannot lump together the Indian and Arabic people. The Indians, I think, like our generosity but dislike anything which savors of bragging about anything we do, because they are traditionally brought up with the idea that a gift is of value only when it is given with as little knowledge by others as possible. The Arabic people, I think, at the present moment are not very fond of any Western foreigners. They tie them up with the colonial domination which they have suffered from. They fear any kind of domination.

My wife and I are going abroad this winter. She is crazy
to visit Spain, but I just can't see it—spending American
dollars in a Fascist country. We both put great stock in
your opinion, Mrs. Roosevelt, and I wish you'd tell us
frankly what you'd do in our position.

I think your wife may be wise in suggesting that you and she should see Spain. In view of the controversy about United States aid to Spain and bases there, it might be well for you to see for yourself what conditions are in that country—whether the Spanish people are content with the present government or wish for a change, and whether or not they can be helped through their government or whether it should be done some other way.

There is much that is beautiful in art and architecture

to see in Spain, and that is important too, but the decision of what the American people should feel about the government of Spain and the conditions now existing there is something worthy of study by every American citizen.

I am a girl of eighteen and worried by my father. He tells me that my ideals about international responsibility for peace are just "book theories," that there has always been war and always will be. He says that now, like the last time, we are going back to isolation. Must this be inevitable? Is he right? If you believe, as I do, that people and nations can change, what would you suggest that I, as one too young to vote, can do about it?

I do not think it is inevitable that we make the same mistakes over and over again. As you read history, you feel that human beings are slow to learn and that our steps forward are often accompanied by waves of retrogression. There is nothing to do, however, but to work for the things in which you believe. You may not be able to vote now, but you can work in the organizations that are trying to bring about the things that you think are right; and in your own life, you can live as you think people should live to bring peace and better citizenship into the world. You will then be prepared to vote more intelligently and to be a better citizen.

Is there anything we can do to convince other countries that not all Americans are money grabbers, strikers and growing isolationists?

Yes. There is a great deal we can do. We can devote ourselves to being good citizens in our communities and to creating public opinion which will make our own community a truly democratic one. If this is so, there will be less isolationism, fewer strikes and the money grabbers will not be very popular. Each one of us can do no more than his share in his own community, but that he must do, or the community will not be part of the whole structure which we hope will be a better world.

What is your opinion of the North Atlantic Pact? Is it a wise move, or are we just looking for trouble?

The North Atlantic Pact is a wise move, I think. At the present there is no force within the United Nations because, until the U.S.S.R. and the U.S.A. come to some kind of understanding on atomic energy, there can be no force set up within the United Nations. Therefore some kind of strength to give security to the smaller nations must be set up. The North Atlantic Pact assures greater security to all those nations belonging to it, since it is a defensive pact and it agrees that if any nation is threatened with aggression the other member nations will immediately consult and take such steps as seem necessary. This should help us to safeguard the peace of the world.

Why does our country lend money and supplies to foreign nations independently of the United Nations?

I suppose you are talking about the Marshall Plan. The reason for it is that under the Charter of the United Nations certain things are permitted, but the budget of the United Nations would not be sufficiently large to cover some of the things which our nation has found it advisable to do. We do them with the full knowledge of the United Nations.

People I know who have been abroad tell me that the "Voice of America" broadcast is known in Europe and Asia as the "Funny Hour" and that, contrary to the impression given to us by the press, the United States is the most unpopular country in the world. If this is so, why is it being concealed from us?

I think the people who told you that the "Voice of America" is known in Europe and Asia as the "Funny Hour" were probably reporting on certain parts of Europe and Asia. I haven't been listening myself with great care, but I heard nothing of the kind when I was in Europe last summer. I can quite imagine, however, that in the Iron Curtain countries and some of the countries of Asia they would try to make fun of these broadcasts to influence the people against them.

I also think that whoever told you the United States was the most unpopular country in the world was exaggerating a good deal. When one nation has a great deal and all the other nations are obliged to ask that nation for help, it is natural that no one who is on the receiving end is very happy. You may see that in your own community if you have anyone there who is well off and has to be constantly appealed to by other people for help. On the other hand, there is recognition of the good that we have done, and gratitude, which I think surpasses their natural feelings of envy and unhappiness which have followed the war.

*Do you think Communist China should have a seat in
the United Nations?*

No, not at the present time. Communist China has
been actively aiding aggression, and until the Korean
question is settled it would be impossible to consider
Communist China as a member of the United Nations.
When peace is restored, then I think a report will have
been made on the qualifications for membership, and
in the light of that report the United Nations members
will have to vote on the admission of Communist China
to the U.N.

*A great deal has been said about the importance of
food in maintaining stable, peaceful conditions. President Truman's Point 4 Program to assist in developing
the productivity of backward areas envisioned better-fed
people in these areas. Would you care to comment on
Point 4 as an aid to peace?*

I think very few people understand the scope of the
Point 4 Program, and yet on its success may depend
much of our future well-being in this country. It is not
relief, it is a program to help people help themselves.
It is providing technical knowledge and American know-
how so that people in underdeveloped, backward areas
will grow more and better quality food, will learn to
market their products so they can buy from us and
from other countries and increase the trade in the
world.

Poverty and starvation are good cradles for communism. It is significant, I think, that the leading democracy
in the world is offering to peoples of backward countries

not relief but the constructive help they need to start their people climbing upward on their own.

In building up Germany to reduce the threat of communism are we forging a weapon which might be turned upon ourselves?

The original policy in connection with Germany, as I understand it, was to try to make her self-supporting. There are, of course, different opinions as to the way in which that should be done. Germany must not be freed from supervision so that she can build up strength for a third world war. It is obvious that whatever she is allowed to build—should she decide that her salvation lay with the communists and not with the democracies— might be used against the democracies and, therefore, against us. She might also try again to build up a superior power in the center of Europe. Only eternal vigilance on the part of those who have had the experience of two world wars begun by Germany will safeguard the world from another war. We certainly should not let Germany, nor anyone else, become a menace to the world as a whole.

21. on the United Nations

Could you tell me about how much the average U.S. citizen pays each year to support the United Nations?

Seventy-four cents a year is the cost per capita. This includes sixteen cents for the specialized agencies.

The United World Federalists are trying to get Congress to have our representatives in the United Nations introduce a proposal to call a convention to amend the United Nations Charter and make the United Nations into a federal world government with limited powers adequate to prevent war. What is your stand with regard to the formation of a world government of this type?

I think we had better work within the United Nations and, through working, discover what is successful and what is not, and make the corrections that are needed in the Charter or in the rules of procedure, according to our practical experience. We may come in time to a world government, but we are not yet prepared for it and too much haste would, I think, be extremely harmful.

I have read that it is difficult for Russia to understand us fully because of differences in our languages which are lost in translation. This is doubtless true of other nations too. Don't you think it would be an excellent idea for the United Nations to push the idea of a common language which every child should be required to master in addition to his own? English has become somewhat of a world language, although it is considered one of the difficult languages to master. Could we not have a simplified English such as Theodore Roosevelt advocated?

I think there is a growing feeling that a common language, learned by all children, would be tremendously advantageous and a help toward peace. The difficulty is that whatever language is chosen, other nations will feel that it gives that nation an added political prestige. You are right; English is becoming more widely known and may, little by little, be accepted as a common language. I doubt very much if simplified English would make a great deal of difference, but a certain amount of simplification is going on all the time.

Why doesn't the United Nations pass a libel law to prevent the poisoning of the minds of the people of one nation against the people of another nation through the use of propaganda in history books, newspapers, radios or movies?

The United Nations does not pass laws. It gets agreement among various nations and they may sign cove-

nants or declarations or treaties. It would be interference
with the freedom of information if you tried to prevent
propaganda or tried to prevent the printing of certain
books and newspapers or the production of certain movies or radio programs because they gave only certain
types of information. The conventions which are de-
signed to insure freedom of information will probably
try to bring about some sort of agreement as to what
type of information can really be considered warmon-
gering and can therefore, by mutual agreement, be
stopped.

*Do you ever regret that New York City was picked as the
site for the United Nations? If I were representing another big power I think I'd resent it very much.*

No, I have never regretted that New York City was
picked as the site of the U.N. The New World was
chosen for the site by a majority U.N. vote because it
was felt to be freer of the jealousies and traditional
methods of doing things than the Old World. New York
City seemed especially suitable because of its reference
libraries and museums. Also, although the U.N. is here,
special U.N. agencies have headquarters in Paris, Rome
and Geneva.

*In a recent newspaper column I read that the United
Nations does not open with prayer, in deference to one
nation's wishes. Do you believe that a meeting of men
without the recognition of divine power can bring the
peace for which we are pleading?*

It seems not to occur to a great many people that the
U.N. is made up of many nations of different religious

faiths. I doubt if any delegate goes to a meeting without a prayer in his heart for guidance in a difficult task, but it would be impossible to demand of a gathering as large as this, with so many different religious practices, that all join in a common prayer. It is not because of deference to one nation's wishes but because of deference to the many nations represented, whose practices and observances vary widely in their respective religions.

What do you think would happen if one of our ships was torpedoed? Would it be handled diplomatically by the United Nations or would it cause an incident similar to the blowing up of the battleship Maine?

I would hope that if one of our ships were torpedoed we would first of all try to get satisfaction through the United Nations. Certainly we should not consider going to war until every other possibility had been exhausted.

What person or nation do you think is making the outstanding contribution to the peace of the world today?

That is a very difficult question to answer, because no one nation by itself could succeed in keeping the peace of the world today. I like to think that our nation, through its willingness to help other nations get back on their own feet in an economic way, has made a real contribution to world peace. But as I look upon the United Nations as the only available machinery we have through which to work for peace, I am constrained to feel that no one contribution would be of much value alone, and therefore the only way we move forward is through the cooperation of the member nations in the agencies that create an atmosphere in which peace can grow.

What can a conference between Russia, the United States and Great Britain accomplish that the United Nations can not?

A conference between Russia, the United States and Great Britain, from my point of view, can accomplish nothing which cannot be accomplished by the United Nations. In fact, I think our only real hope of accomplishing anything is through the United Nations, because I believe we have reached a point at present where we need the impact of the opinion of the world on this whole question of the control of armaments and the complete wiping out of the fear of world destruction.

Do you think the U.N. is becoming progressively stronger? Do you feel that within our generation more power will be given to it and that through the U.N. world peace may become a reality?

I should say that the U.N. has become progressively stronger in the past four years. Every year sees better understanding developing among the vast majority of the nations represented. We are learning gradually to work together. The only people with whom we haven't in any way been able to improve our relations are the people in the U.S.S.R. That is because there is a deep suspicion on both sides and an inability to talk to one another except as government representatives, which does not lead to greater understanding. I think, however, as understanding grows with other nations throughout the world we may break down some of the suspicions.

No more power can be given the U.N. until we and the U.S.S.R. can come to some kind of agreement to live in the same world together, each pursuing our own way of life but at least having economic and cultural contacts which may help us to greater understanding of each other. When we achieve this I think world peace can become a reality.

Our local paper has published several editorials stating that UNESCO is a Communist organization. Will you please tell me how much truth there is in this accusation?

Since the Soviets refuse to belong to UNESCO, it is difficult to see how it could be under their domination.

Isolationists who do not want international cooperation are inclined to call everything Communistic, and they use this label to harm all the efforts of the UN and its specialized agencies. I am quite sure that neither UNESCO nor any other UN agency at the present time has been taken over by Communists.

22. on My Husband

Do you think your husband had any premonition that he might not live to complete his last term in the White House?

No, I do not think my husband had any premonition that he would not live to finish his term in the White House. Four years previously I think he had a feeling that any man well might not live through a third term. But, having lived through the third term, he believed, I think, that if it was right for him to run he would be able to win and he would live as long as he was needed to do his work.

Would you tell me what books and authors your illustrious husband most frequently mentioned as having influenced his vision and action?

I am afraid he never mentioned books in this connection. He always talked of Mahan's Naval History as having been one of the books which he found most illuminating when he read it. He liked historical biographies primarily, and read very widely.

He had a very catholic interest in many subjects, and of course read a great deal of history, though I do not remember hearing him say at any time that particular writings or particular books had influenced his point of view. I should say that Woodrow Wilson had a great influence upon him, and Theodore Roosevelt, partly in their writings and much as individuals. My husband frequently talked about them, but not as inspirations.

I have just read F. D. R.: His Personal Letters. In one or two letters he refers to his engagement to you but says nothing about how or when you became engaged. If this isn't too intimate a subject, I'd like to know a little more about how and where this happened.

I became engaged to my husband on a weekend which we spent at Groton School, where we were visiting my young brother. I imagine, since my husband was writing personal letters, he thought that anyone concerned would probably know when we became engaged.

You remarked in your column recently that the "work as usual" way Governor Dewey spent his birthday didn't seem a very happy way of celebrating the occasion. I thought your husband was a "work as usual" man on his birthday too. Am I wrong?

My husband always had to work during the day on his birthday because he was always engaged in work that could not be laid aside, but his birthday was a day of much celebration. There was family celebration in the morning before going to work, and every year we had a particular group of friends who celebrated with him at dinner and in the evening.

Was your husband a regular churchgoer?

My husband was senior warden in our church at Hyde Park when he died. He went to church as often as it was possible for him to do so. It was extremely difficult for him to do this regularly in the last years of his life, and therefore I could not say that he was a regular churchgoer, but he performed his duties as senior warden and was extremely interested always in the church.

Is it true that your husband, the late President Roosevelt, never wrote his own speeches?

No. My husband wrote a great many speeches in his own hand. When he became President, however, he developed a regular routine. First of all he decided on the subject with which he was going to deal, then he called in the Government officials charged with the responsibility for the work on this particular subject: for instance, if it was to be a fiscal speech, the Treasury Department and the Federal Reserve Board were consulted; if agriculture, the Department of Agriculture and allied agencies, and so on.

After he had all the facts, he usually sat down with two or three people and explained his ideas of what he wished said. They made a first draft and brought it back to him. He then went over it, and sometimes there were as many as six or eight or ten drafts of the same speech. One member of this small group was usually someone adept at phrasing, another was good at cutting, because in any speech which is made over the radio one is apt to put a great deal too much into it to fit the time. In between each rewriting my husband went over it again, and if you ever go to the library at Hyde Park you will see the collection of speeches with corrections on the various copies in my husband's own handwriting.

When a speech was finally written, my husband always practically knew every word that was in it by heart, as he had gone over it so often. It was the final expression of his original thoughts. I have, however, seen my husband take a speech which his advisers thought was completely finished, tear it up and dictate an entirely new speech because he felt it was not simple and clear enough. He retained the facts, but he was particularly adept at putting thoughts into simple and clear enough words so that even I, who might not know anything on the subject, found I could comprehend what he was talking about.

They say that many great men's wives have a feeling of intuition, before the men become well known, that their husbands are marked for greatness. Did you have any feeling like that about your husband when you were first married?

No, but I am not given to going much beyond the things that have to be done each day. I have always been so busy that, if I thought I had adequately met the demands day by day, what was going to happen in the future never received a great deal of thought.

It is a mystery to me how a man from a conservative, wealthy home like Mr. Roosevelt ever became such a

*great liberal. What do you think influenced him most in
this direction?*

> Very often a social conscience is more easily awakened
> in one who has not been hardened by having to battle
> for every advantage in life. My husband's parents brought
> him up with a sense of obligation to other people. He
> had a chance to travel and make contact in a simple way
> with people in other parts of the world. His mind was
> open and intelligent, and as his contacts broadened his
> sense of justice deepened. He was a liberal because he
> believed in social justice.

*What people besides President Roosevelt's parents and
yourself had the most important personal influence on
his life?*

> I think Louis Howe had a great influence on my hus-
> band's life, and also his two uncles, Mr. Warren Delano
> and Mr. Frederic Delano—and my uncle, Theodore
> Roosevelt, made a deep impression on him as a young
> man, as he did on so many other young men of that
> generation.

*What did President Roosevelt plan to do when he retired
from the Presidency to private life again?*

> My husband had planned when he retired to write regu-
> larly for one magazine and to devote himself to putting
> his papers in order and to enlarging and making more
> interesting the library at Hyde Park.

*Your husband never wrote pointed personal letters, as
President Truman does, but he certainly must have
needed to let off steam at times. What kind of safety*

valve did he have in periods of terrible tension and pressure?

My husband disliked writing longhand letters, except for brief business or personal memos. Temperaments differ. He was very slow to anger, but when he was angry it shook him to the bottom of his soul and he was more apt to take his anger out in cold and never-to-be-forgotten words than in any impulsive way.

To the ordinary criticism affecting him and his family he rarely paid any attention. He taught us all to believe that it was better to ignore criticism. He lost respect for some writers and critics and then rarely read what they said, so, of course, they bothered him little. He also advised us to look with care for any constructive criticism, but if it became particularly carping to ignore it and never answer it.

His illness had given him extraordinary self-control in personal matters. When matters affecting affairs of the country were at stake, and in periods of tension and pressure, he practiced this same self-control. He suffered when things went wrong with the family, though those personal things were quickly swallowed up in the much more important things that touched the country as a whole.

Did your husband ever describe his personal impressions of Stalin? I seem to have heard that they got on very well, exchanged jokes, etc.

Yes. When my husband came home he always talked over his trip. When he came home from his first meeting with Mr. Stalin in Tehran, he told us he sensed a great suspicion on the part of the Marshal but formal relations were always polite. He felt no warmth of understanding or of normal intercourse. My husband determined to bend every effort to breaking these suspicions down, and decided that the way to do it was to live up to every promise made by both the United States and Great Britain, which both of us were able to do before the Yalta meeting.

At Yalta my husband felt the atmosphere had somewhat cleared, and he did say he was able to get a smile from Stalin.

I understand that President Roosevelt used to have a couple of cocktails before dinner. What did he drink?

I do not think that my husband often had a couple of cocktails before dinner. Sometimes he did, but not always, and many times he had none. When he made cocktails, he liked a Martini, a rum cocktail or an Old-Fashioned. It was more a question with him of a time to relax and have a few friendly minutes with people than of caring very much what he drank or even whether he had a drink. The doctors approved of it because they thought it helped his circulation.

We would like to serve your husband's favorite menu at a dinner to open the polio drive and commemorate his birthday on January 30. Could you tell us some of his favorite dishes?

My husband was very fond of curried chicken. He also liked scrambled eggs, corned-beef hash or roast-beef hash, any kind of game and especially terrapin, Maryland style. Waffles with maple syrup was a favorite dessert.

Which of the books about your husband do you feel
gives the most accurate picture of him, and which the
least accurate?

If you are interested in my husband's labor record, Miss
Frances Perkins' book, *The Roosevelt I Knew*, is excellent. *Roosevelt and Hopkins*, by Mr. Robert Sherwood,
gives an extraordinarily good picture of the general times.
Perhaps my husband's own letters, edited by my son
Elliott, would give you a more intimate picture of his
personality than anything else. The book I like least,
and which is the least accurate, is John T. Flynn's; but,
of course, there are many books about my husband
which I have not had time to read.

In This I Remember *you stated that our late President*
was advised to eliminate the famous "stab in the back"
from his speech after Mussolini attacked France, and that
he refused to do so. Miss Grace Tully said that it was not
in the President's script and that he ad libbed it. Which
of you is right?

Miss Tully is quite right. The phrase "stab in the back"
was not in the President's script. It had been discussed
beforehand, and his advisers urged him not to put it in.
He put it in on his own initiative when he was making
his speech. He did this sort of thing quite often, so there
is nothing contradictory between what Miss Tully said
and what I said.

I wish to know if the quotation "We have nothing to
fear but fear itself" is an original saying of the late Presi-
dent. If not, from whom did he quote?

It was an original saying, if there is anything really original!

Do you feel that your opinions ever changed your husband's political decisions?
Never.

23. on Myself

What single accomplishment in your life are you proud-
est of?

I never thought of being proud of anything. As I look back I think the thing that gave me the greatest satisfaction was finally learning to swim. I was so afraid of the water that conquering that fear was a great satisfaction.

When did you first start writing for newspapers and
magazines? Did you have any particular models among
the columnists when you started?

In the late 1920s. I cannot remember that I had a model columnist. I admired the writings of Robert Louis Stevenson, and I had read widely as a young person, but I did not have any particular model.

For the fourth time the American Institute of Public
Opinion's annual admiration "derby" was won by you,

*Mrs. Roosevelt. I'd like your honest opinion. What do
you think is the reason for this popularity?*

I did not know the American Institute of Public Opinion's annual admiration "derby" was won by me. But I am afraid that I bask in reflected glory. It was probably won because of the abiding love and admiration for my husband. He was able to do many things for many people during his lifetime, and in this particular case they have not had time to forget; so that when my nomination comes up I rejoice in the kind feelings he left behind. In addition, I have tried to go on with some of of the work which he began. In the U.S., I think, there is always recognition of a genuine effort to continue doing something useful.

*Do you miss the comings and goings, the hustle-bustle
routine you followed when Mr. Roosevelt was in the
Presidency?*

No. I cannot say that I miss the hustle-bustle routine or the comings and goings that were part of my life when I lived in the White House. I never have lived a very quiet life, and I cannot say that life is very quiet today. I keep busy enough so that I have very little time for wishing life might be something different.

Has the fact that you were born to wealth and have always enjoyed luxuries that are denied to many, through no fault of their own, ever bothered your conscience? Or do you feel justified in not sharing it?

I wonder what makes you feel I have always enjoyed luxuries. I have always had a home, but when I was young it was not my own and I had a great sense of obligation to my grandmother and aunts and uncles who took me in. I probably worried about money more than most youngsters because my grandmother never let me know whether I could have anything, and frequently I could not have the things I really wanted most. I have seen many youngsters in far poorer homes who had many more things than I had when I was young.

As to the last part of your question, I do not know what you call sharing. Everyone pays the Government a tax on income, and that is shared with the people as a whole. As I have made more money my obligations have grown and all I have is "shared" with others, so I do not really think my conscience ever troubles me.

I suppose every new first lady must worry about making mistakes. Do you feel you made any serious ones during your first year in the White House?

I am afraid I am not the one to pick out what serious mistakes I made. Plenty of people have picked them out and mentioned them, but I did not always happen to agree that the things to which people objected were mistakes, so this is a question you will have to ask some-one else.

I can tell you one thing I did that horrified the head usher, Mr. Ike Hoover, and that was running the electric elevator myself. He thought that very undignified and an unpardonable sin. However, before I left the White House it was accepted as a perfectly normal procedure.

In photographs of your home I have never noticed any modern furniture or paintings. Is this because you dislike them?

Not at all. We have lived at home always with things that have been in the family for years. Outside of buying a comfortable chair or two now and then, I cannot remember buying any furniture for many years, so I am accustomed to rooms which are filled with old-fashioned things.

Was Franklin Roosevelt your first girlhood sweetheart?

Of course not, unless you consider one's first girlhood sweetheart the first young man one ever knew. I imagine my husband was the first person I remember, since I met him when I was two and he was a little over three.

Are you financially dependent on what you make from magazines, radio, etc., or do you have a private income?

I have a private income. I would, however, have to live very differently from the way I live at present, and cut out doing a great many things that I now do, if I were not earning money. Therefore, as long as I can work I shall continue to do so and earn money, as I enjoy being able to give away some money and to keep open house and to serve in various organizations. I especially like to be able to travel. All these preferences of mine are expensive preferences, but I have the security of knowing that I can live on my income when I have to do so, even though my style of living will be much more restricted.

When you were a little girl what did you most want to be when you grew up?

First, I wanted above all to be a trained nurse. Later, above all I wanted to be able to sing and have a beautiful voice which would move people. I achieved the first ambition when my children were small. I became a good nurse under the direction of a real trained nurse who spent a great deal of time with me in those days. I never achieved the second desire, not having been gifted with any voice at all.

You—having had an excellent background, a wonderful education, an unlimited amount of parliamentary experience, so many years in the White House, so many positions of note, and having had an honest political career all your life, with a real human heart—why then do you not do the world a favor by running for the office of President of the United States, thereby becoming the first female President and demonstrating what a Roosevelt can do?

You credit me, my dear lady, with more qualifications than I believe I have. You also forget that I am 68 years of age and that I have no desire to be President of the United States.

I do not think the time has come for a woman to be President of the United States. It seems to me that before a woman can successfully be President many more public offices must be filled by women and we in this country must have ceased to think of our candidates as men or women but only as people who have the proper qualifications for the job to which we are considering electing them.

On the whole I think the Roosevelts have already demonstrated what they can do, and probably will do so many times again, but I do not think it is up to me to demonstrate either the capacities of Roosevelts or women in general. I feel at the present time that a woman could not fill the Presidency successfully because she might not be able to hold a following long enough, and without a loyal following she could accomplish little.

If you had been a man what career would you have chosen to pursue?

I haven't the remotest idea. I cannot imagine what it would be like to be a man, nor to have the choice of a career. Therefore I have never had the slightest desire to think about what I would have done.

What do you do with mail you do not like?

I do not often have mail which I do not like, but I sometimes have critical mail. If I think a letter is honest and reasonable I answer it. Occasionally I think it would not serve any good purpose to answer it, so I simply do not answer it. I have always kept a file of disagreeable letters, which I call my "hair shirt" file, so that in case at any time I should feel the nice letters were giving me too much satisfaction I would always have something to turn to to keep my feet reasonably safely on the ground.

If you had a choice of spending your last years anywhere in the world, where would it be?

In my own home at Hyde Park in Dutchess County, New York.

When, if ever, have you admitted that you've been wrong about something?

It seems to me I have to admit that every day. All of us are wrong about certain things, but we have to act on our convictions. If we are wrong we usually learn about it sooner or later.

At what age do you hope to retire from public life?
    I never plan ahead.

24. on Gossip

What is your answer to the statement about your husband which appears in Jesse Jones's memoirs: "Regardless of his oft-repeated statement, 'I hate war,' he was eager to get into the fighting, since that would insure a third term"?

This statement could not possibly be true. The most elementary thing in human nature is the desire to protect one's children. Mr. Jones had no children who would inevitably have to go to war. My husband knew full well that if war came our four sons not only would go to war but would ask to have waived many of the physical defects which kept others out of the war, so that they might go into more dangerous places.

I have heard over and over again that your husband had already had a cerebral hemorrhage and was a very sick man before he accepted the nomination for a fourth term. Will you tell me the truth about this?

As far as I know that is utterly false. I have asked the doctor who watched him carefully, and from my own observation I cannot see how it would have been possible for my husband to have had anything of this kind without someone noticing it. He had a thorough examination before he ran for a fourth term, and the doctors said that if he would follow certain rules there was no indication that he could not stand the strain of another term in office.

I read an article by Westbrook Pegler in which he stated that Mr. Roosevelt "signed his name to a property deed at his real-estate promotion at Warm Springs, Georgia, forbidding forever the sale of his land to any Afro, or its rental or occupancy by any such." If the statement is correct, how do you reconcile the inconsistencies of the Roosevelt family in relation to their public utterances and private actions?

I know nothing of the property deeds signed by my husband in Warm Springs. I do realize, however, that in signing a deed he would have been obliged to conform to the laws of the state in which that deed was signed. If the state of Georgia has any such laws as you mention, he would have been obliged to sign in order to obtain the land. Since the property passed out of my husband's hands very soon after he acquired it, as he sold it to the Foundation, I have never heard much about the conditions under which the land was acquired or sold.

Why didn't President Roosevelt buy any War Savings Bonds?

He did, but he bought them for our children and grandchildren and gave them to them immediately. My understanding is that he bought to the limit on each issue.

There is a story, unfortunately widely current, that President Roosevelt's coffin was opened before burial to one person only—Mr. Molotov. I have tried to refute this story, but I am now asking you to tell me whether it is true or not true.

These rumors always seem strange to me. My husband and I had talked on various occasions of our dislike for the usual lying-in-state which public servants usually were subjected to, and it was his wish that the coffin be closed as soon as possible. It was left open after we reached the White House long enough for me to go and place a few flowers where I wished them to be. The ushers and the people who had duties to perform were the only ones who saw the coffin open, as our children who were at home at that time preferred to remember their father as they had known him.

This story of Mr. Molotov's having seen the coffin open is utterly ridiculous. I do not even remember whether Mr. Molotov was in this country. He may have been, but as far as I am concerned, I have no idea who among the diplomats attended the funeral services, and certainly no one of them saw the coffin open.

Did you or your husband ever take any steps to stop the gossip and unkind comments that were circulated about you while you were in Washington?

No. In a way I think one is very fortunate in the White House. One is cut off in so many ways there from the ordinary social contacts of life that gossip of this kind

seldom comes to one's attention immediately. One does
learn eventually, of course, what is being said.

The other day a party made the statement that Presi-
dent Roosevelt received a $10,000 salary from the March
of Dimes. Is that so or not?

That is not true. My husband never received any salary
from the National Foundation for Infantile Paralysis
or from the March of Dimes. If you will read my book
you will get the whole financial picture of how Warm
Springs was started. The National Foundation for Infantile Paralysis took out a large life insurance policy
later so that after my husband's death his estate would
be reimbursed for the money which he lent for the
establishment of Warm Springs and which they had
not been able to pay back.

Is it true that you and Franklin were separated at the
time he was first nominated for President and became
reconciled for appearance's sake for campaign purposes?

This same story has been circulated about nearly every
President and his wife, and I am surprised that anybody
believes it any more. I was never separated from my husband.

In the book called Jim Farley's Own Story *he claims you*
made the remark: "... my husband never felt com-
fortable or at ease unless he was with people of his own
social class and standing." Is that true?

I never made the remark attributed to me by Mr. Farley
in his book. I may have said something which he interpreted as meaning what he has put down, but what-

ever I may have said had a different meaning to me from the one which he has placed upon it. My husband got on with all kinds of people, and among the friends he enjoyed the most were people who certainly did not have the same educational or social background.

An editorial in the Tulsa Tribune says that your husband "declared frankly" when he took us into the United Nations "that he didn't see how it would work." Is there any truth in this?

I cannot imagine that my husband ever said anything of the kind. He had a great belief that the United Nations could work. I would like to point out to you that my husband did not take the United States into the U.N. He appointed representatives to go to San Francisco, but he was dead before the meeting was held. They drew up a charter, and our Senate ratified it, so you can hardly say that my husband took us into the U.N.

Several people have told me that, from the very time your five children were born, you had help and never bathed one of them yourself or fed them or put them to bed, or even pinned a diaper. I do not believe this, as I don't think there is a mother, no matter how much help she has, who would not want the pleasure of doing some of these things. If you will answer this question, then that story will be settled for good.

I did have help from the time my children were born. However, every mother, I think, at times takes complete charge of her children, and I was no different from any other mother. Every mother, for the reason you give, would miss a great part of the joy of motherhood if she did not bathe and dress and feed her own children. I did all these things every day of my life when my children were growing up, and I became a good trained nurse in the course of the years and nursed my family through various contagious diseases and serious illnesses.

During your late husband's administration as President you were generally regarded as the leader, or champion, of the communist elements. It has been proved that you assisted the Eislers, Browders, Lashes and other well-known Commies. According to recent press reports, you seem to have lost your enthusiasm for communism. Would you tell us why?

It is interesting to me that you say it has been proved that I aided the Eislers, Browders, Lashes and other well-known Communists. That statement is entirely false.

In the first place, Joseph Lash is not a Communist and never was one. He started the Students' Union and was put out of it when the communist element took control, and then he aided the opposition forces. I never knew the Eislers, but when I was in the White House I received innumerable requests to help people. I forwarded the letters to the State Department with the usual request which was well understood: "Could this be looked into?" This only means review to find out if anything improper had been done.

Browder's case was similar. I know of no well-known Communists whom I ever assisted in any way, or any other Communists.

There were young people in the youth movement who were Communists and with whom I worked. Whether they are Communists today or not, I do not know.

These were times which were very hard for young people, and one had to look for ways in which to make them feel they had some hope under a democracy, if they were to become good citizens in the future. I never had any enthusiasm for communism, any more than I have today. Naturally things are often stated by people who desire to make political capital out of them, but they are untrue.

I realize that no person who has accomplished as much for the good of our nation as you have could help but step on a few toes. This is where the malicious rumor I am constantly hearing must have had its origin. It is generally believed in this part of the country that you are part Negro and that is why you are taking up for them. Could you manage to let them know the truth?

Anyone who cares to look into the genealogy of the Roosevelts—and I happen to be descended from the Theodore Roosevelt side of the family—can also look into the collateral branches and can find the answer to your question. As far as I know, I have no Negro blood; but I suppose if any of us could trace our ancestry back far enough we would find that in the tribes from which we are all originally descended, all kinds of blood is mixed. It always seems quite foolish to me to begin to wonder what strains you might have beyond those you actually know about!

I envy you your disposition on being able to keep quiet when annoyed. In my case, I blow off my top. Then I'm sorry; and I don't like to do anything I'm sorry for,

either. I have noticed that many people send you some
awful digs. You answer them so nice and polite. How
can you do it?

 I suppose because they really do not annoy me. When
you have lived to my age and have been in the public
eye for so long, it is only the people whom you love
who can really hurt or annoy you. You may be influenced by what other people say if you think their criticisms are reasonable and valid, but you do not get either
hurt or annoyed. You also know that many things are said
for political reasons or out of jealousy or ignorance or
spite. Time disproves them and usually they carry little
weight.

We have had a scandal in our family involving our old-
est daughter. It takes all my strength now just to face my
neighbors. How do people in public life, like yourself,
keep your balance and courage with all the gossiping
and backbiting that goes on about you and your fami-
lies?

 I suppose people in public life are so accustomed to gossip they become rather indifferent, because they have to
survive so much that is untrue. In your case—if you fully
understand what happened, and if you feel that there
are reasons which explain human frailties, and if you do
not yourself feel bitterly toward your daughter but love
her and want to help her through what is probably for
her a bitter and difficult experience—I would feel, as I
have always felt, that gossip and backbiting are matters
of utter indifference. There is only one important thing,
and that is to help a human being through whatever

experience or mistake he or she has made to become a stronger and better person in the future.

If your friends do not help, then they are not real friends, so what difference does it make what they say or how they feel?